MUSHROOM RECIPES

MUSHROOM RECIPES

Countess Morphy

ARC BOOKS, INC.
New York

Published 1966 by ARC BOOKS, Inc.
219 Park Avenue South, New York, N.Y. 10003

Foreword

BY JOSEPH L. HYDE *

This cook book is for the artistic, creative cook, not for those who are slaves to the measuring cup, meat thermometer, teaspoons and tablespoons. What you'll get is hundreds of wonderful ideas about cooking mushrooms. Of course the measurements are accurate but in any recipe they should be incidental to the total concept of the dish in question.

The mushroom, with such exquisite taste, deserves anthems of praise. (An Anthem to Mycology was performed recently at the New York Mycological Society's Annual banquet.) For the knowledgeable mycologist or toadstool hunters many of the recipes in this book could be made using wild mushrooms.

Countess Morphy has paid great attention to such basic recipes as Duxelle, so indispensable to French

---

*Mr. Hyde, member of the New York Mycological Society, has been chef to the society's banquet ever since its founding in 1962.

cooking. Her Sole Bonne Femme is accurate, feasible, and I think it is one of the pinnacles of French gastronomy.

I credit Countess Morphy for having written a fine mushroom cook book. I credit her doubly for involving in her recipes a profusion of the mushroom's best friends, lemon juice and dear butter.

"Old Library"   Joseph Hyde
Palisades, New Jersey

Contents

8

CONTENTS

SAUCES WITH MUSHROOMS

PART II—DISHES WITH MUSHROOMS

MUSHROOM SOUPS

FISH

MEAT

POULTRY

GAME

Introduction

THE mushroom has been the joy of the epicure throughout the ages, and if its more aristocratic underground cousin, the truffle, has earned the title of the "black diamond of cookery," the mushroom well deserves to rank as the precious "pearl of cookery." It is one of the most useful and delicious members of the vegetable kingdom, and not only does it constitute the principal ingredient in many excellent dishes, but it is an indispensable adjunct to many others; as a flavouring it is essential in all good cookery.

Fortunately, mushrooms are no longer a luxury in this country, and their cultivation is now an established and growing industry, with the result that prices have fallen, and this valuable fungus is within the reach of both rich and poor.

The mushroom-lover will find in this book a variety of dishes which are simple and easy to prepare and cook, and most of them are designed to enhance the delicate aroma and taste of the "pearl of cookery."

MUSHROOM
RECIPES

The Choice and Preparation of Mushrooms

MUSHROOMS should be very fresh, and when fresh they are of a good colour, quite firm and not fully open. When mushrooms are to be used as a garnish, the small button variety are the best, and they should be chosen as white as possible. Brown mushrooms are considered by some to have a stronger and better flavour than white mushrooms; but on the other hand, the white mushrooms have, perhaps, a more delicate aroma. This is very much a question of individual taste.

To prepare mushrooms for cooking, trim off neatly the tip of the stalk, and lightly scrape the stalk. Of, if preferred—and for certain dishes this is necessary—remove the stalk altogether. Throw the mushrooms in a large basin of cold water, and rub them lightly and rapidly with the hands. Remove them from the water, and wash them again in clean water in the same manner. Leave them as little time as possible in the water, as they lose their flavour and become limp. *Mushrooms should never be allowed to stand in water*, and should never be washed in warm or hot water. Now drain them on a sieve or in a cloth, peel them and cook at once. Another golden rule is that mushrooms should not be prepared and peeled beforehand, but only just before they are going to be cooked.

The most satisfactory way of peeling small or button mushrooms, is to peel them as one does an apple, in a circular or spiral way. The mushroom is held in the left hand and turned and peeled with a small sharp knife. Done in this manner, and with a little experience, the mushroom is quite smooth, and shows no mark from the knife.

The larger or more fully-opened mushrooms are easier to peel umbrella-wise from the edges towards the centre.

Mushroom peelings and stalks should never be thrown away. They can be chopped and used as flavouring for sauces, soups, etc.

PART I

Mushroom Dishes

BAKED MUSHROOMS (Austrian)

Choose as far as is possible, mushrooms of equal size. Peel them and remove the stalks. Put the mushrooms in a well-buttered glass fireproof dish, which has a lid, cover with sour cream, season with salt, pepper and a good squeeze of lemon juice and bake in a moderate oven for 25 to 30 minutes, according to the size of the mushrooms. Remove the lid only when serving.

CANAPÉS À LA DUXELLES

Cut neat rounds of bread, about 2½ inches in diameter and just under ½ inch thick and toast them. Spread with a thick layer of Duxelles Sauce (see p. 64), sprinkle with cheese and brown lightly under the grill or in a brisk oven.

CHOPPED MUSHROOMS ON TOAST

Peel the mushrooms and remove the stalks. Chop both mushrooms and stalks coarsely, and cook in a little hot butter for 8 to 10 minutes, seasoning with salt, cayenne pepper and a good squeeze of lemon juice. When done, spread on neat rounds or triangles of toasted bread, sprinkle with a little chopped parsley and serve very hot.

"CROQUETS" OF MUSHROOMS

Peel and chop finely $\frac{1}{2}$ lb. of mushrooms, and cook in butter, as in the foregoing recipe. Then mix with a few tablespoons of thick Mornay Sauce (see p. 70), and let stand till quite cold. Have ready a few slices of bread, just under $\frac{1}{2}$ inch thick and about 3 inches square, and fry these to a light golden colour in butter. Cover each with the mushroom mixture, brush over with lightly-beaten yolk of egg, sprinkle freely with very fine white breadcrumbs and fry in hot butter or oil, basting frequently, so that the top of the "croquets" will be lightly browned. Drain and serve very hot.

CROÛTES WITH MUSHROOMS

Cut rounds of bread 3 inches in diameter and $\frac{1}{2}$ inch thick. Stamp out of each, and in the centre, rounds of $1\frac{1}{2}$ inches in diameter, but being careful not to cut through the bread. Fry to a light golden colour in butter, and remove the centre round. This will leave a hollow. Fill each case with small mushrooms cooked as for Mushrooms as a Garnish (p. 38) and afterwards mixed with a little Poulette Sauce (see p. 66).

CROÛTES WITH MUSHROOMS À L'ORLÉANS

Cook some button mushrooms in a little butter, seasoning with salt and pepper and adding a little cream and 1 tablespoon of Madeira. When done, put a few in small cases of puff pastry, which have been sprinkled with grated cheese. Put in a brisk oven and serve as soon as they begin to brown.

CURRIED MUSHROOMS

Fry 2 or 3 sliced onions in butter to a golden brown, add $\frac{1}{2}$ lb. of chopped tomatoes, and simmer gently till the tomatoes are reduced to a pulp. Sprinkle with 2 heaped teaspoons of curry powder and 1 level teaspoon of salt. Mix thoroughly and simmer for another 5 minutes. Then add $\frac{1}{2}$ pint of stock or water, bring to the boil and simmer for 20 minutes, adding a little more stock or water, if the sauce appears too thick. Now add about $\frac{3}{4}$ lb. of peeled mushrooms, left whole if they are of medium size, or quartered if large. Mix thoroughly with the sauce and simmer for 15 to 20 minutes, till the mushrooms are tender.

DEVILLED MUSHROOMS

Put 1 teaspoon of finely-chopped shallot or onion in a small saucepan with 6 tablespoons of tarragon vinegar, 3 of dry white wine (optional) and reduce by half on a quick fire. Add $\frac{1}{2}$ pint of good stock, $\frac{1}{2}$ oz. of butter worked with $\frac{1}{2}$ oz. of flour and stir well. Season with 1 teaspoon of made mustard, salt and a dash of cayenne. Simmer for 10 minutes. Then put the sauce in a larger saucepan, add ½ lb. or more of peeled mushrooms, previously lightly cooked in butter, stir well and simmer for a few minutes, without boiling.

FLAN OF MUSHROOMS

Line a flan tin with puff pastry or short crust, cover with small mushrooms cooked as for a Garnish (see p. 38) and mixed with a few tablespoons of cold Béchamel Sauce (see p. 69). Decorate the flan with thin bands of pastry, forming a trellis. Brush these over with beaten yolk of egg and bake in a fairly brisk oven till the pastry is lightly coloured. Serve very hot.

FRIED MUSHROOMS À LA RUSSE

Peel the mushrooms, but do not remove the stalks—they should be neatly trimmed only. Season with salt, then dip each in flour, coat with beaten yolk of egg, then with fine white breadcrumbs and fry in butter—preferably clarified butter—to a light golden colour. Drain, put on a hot dish, sprinkle with a little chopped fennel, and serve very hot with quartered lemons on a separate dish.

FRICASSÉE OF MUSHROOMS À LA COMTOISE

Cut ¼ lb. of gammon into small dice and brown lightly in butter, with 1 large onion, coarsely chopped. Cook to a golden colour, and add 3 gills of either boiling stock or water and $\frac{3}{4}$ lb. of thinly-sliced mushrooms. Season with salt and pepper, add a good pinch of chopped thyme, parsley, marjoram and 1 tablespoon of butter. Mix all thoroughly. Simmer for 20 to 30 minutes, and serve very hot.

FRICASSÉE OF MUSHROOMS WITH CREAM

Put 1 lb. of small, peeled mushrooms in a saucepan with $2\frac{1}{2}$ ozs. of butter, and cook, but without browning. Sprinkle with 1 tablespoon of flour and season with salt, pepper, a pinch of allspice and sprinkle with chopped parsley. Mix the yolks of 2 eggs in a basin with a little over $\frac{1}{2}$ pint of cream, seasoning with salt and pepper and pour this over the mushrooms. Mix thoroughly and, when very hot, but not boiling, remove from the fire. Add the juice of $\frac{1}{2}$ a lemon and serve on a hot dish.

FRICASSÉE OF MUSHROOMS WITH PARMESAN CHEESE

Proceed as in the foregoing recipe, but add 2 tablespoons of grated Parmesan cheese to the cream and egg mixture.

GRILLED MUSHROOMS

Choose somewhat large mushrooms of equal size. Wash and dry them carefully; peel them, remove the stalks, season lightly with salt and pepper and brush them over with oil. Put them on a hot oiled or buttered grill and do not grill too quickly. When done, put them on a hot dish or serve them on hot buttered toast. They can also be served with the top downwards, and on each is placed a soft pat of Maître d'Hôtel butter, made as follows: Work butter and finely-chopped parsley to a smooth paste, allowing 1 level teaspoon of parsley to every 2 ozs. of butter, and seasoning with salt, pepper and a good squeeze of lemon juice. Roll into small pats.

GRILLED MUSHROOMS À LA BORDELAISE

Choose large mushrooms and remove the stalks. Chop the latter finely and cook in a little butter and white wine with chopped shallot and parsley, seasoning with salt and pepper. Prepare and grill the mushrooms as in preceding recipe. To serve, put the mushrooms on a hot dish with the top downwards and put on each a little of the chopped stalks, etc.

GRILLED MUSHROOMS À LA BOURGUIGNONNE

Proceed as in the foregoing recipe, but cook the stalks in a little red wine, instead of white, and add a pinch of chopped thyme, parsley and $\frac{1}{2}$ a small bayleaf. Let the sauce reduce till thick and put a little of the mixture on each grilled mushroom.

GRILLED MUSHROOMS WITH PAPRIKA BUTTER

Grill the mushrooms as in foregoing recipes, but garnish with a pat of Paprika Butter, made as follows: Allow 1 teaspoon of Paprika—Paprika is a very mild Hungarian red pepper—to every 2 ozs. of butter, mix and work to a smooth paste.

GRILLED MUSHROOMS AND SAUSAGES

Grill some large mushrooms as in foregoing recipes, and on each mushroom place 2 or 3 grilled midget sausages. Season with a good dash of pepper just before serving. The mushrooms can also be served on hot buttered toast with the sausages as a garnish.

MUSHROOMS WITH ANCHOVY BUTTER

Peel the mushrooms and toss for 10 minutes or longer, according to their size, in hot butter, seasoning with a little pepper. Five minutes before serving add 2 tablespoons of Anchovy Butter made as follows: Allow 4 anchovies (in brine), or 6 or 8 small fillets of anchovy in oil, to every 2 ozs. of butter. When anchovies in brine are used, they should be thoroughly washed in cold water and well dried in a cloth. Pound them to a smooth paste in a mortar, add the butter and pound and mix with the anchovies. Rub through a sieve into a basin and stir with a wooden spoon.

MUSHROOMS À L'ARLÉSIENNE

To each lb. of mushrooms, allow $\frac{1}{2}$ lb. of tomatoes. Peel the mushrooms and quarter them if they are large. Quarter the tomatoes. Put the mushrooms and tomatoes in a well-buttered fireproof dish, sprinkle with 1 teaspoon of chopped shallot or onion, 1 of parsley, the juice of $\frac{1}{2}$ a lemon and season with salt and pepper. Sprinkle with 1 or 2 tablespoons of olive oil and bake in a quick oven for 20 minutes or longer, according to the size of the mushrooms.

MUSHROOM AND BACON SAVOURY

Choose medium-sized mushrooms, peel them and remove the stalks. Cook in the same manner as Mushrooms for Garnish (see p. 38) and, when done, drain thoroughly and dry. Wrap each mushroom in a thin rasher of bacon—or 2 or 3 mushrooms, if they are small—fasten with a skewer, and either grill, or fry in hot butter. To serve, put on rounds of hot buttered toast, remove the skewer and serve very hot.

MUSHROOMS À LA BARIGOULE

Choose large mushrooms of equal size. Peel them and remove the stalks. Cook them in hot butter for 10 to 15 minutes, according to their size, seasoning with salt and pepper. When done, arrange neatly on a hot dish, pour a little of the butter in which they were cooked over them, and cover each mushroom with a layer of thick Duxelles Sauce (see p. 64), to which cooked diced gammon has been added.

MUSHROOMS À LA BÉCHAMEL

Wash and peel the mushrooms, and if large quarter them. Cook for 10 to 15 minutes in Béchamel Sauce (see p. 69), according to their size, and just before serving add 1 teaspoon of lemon juice and a dash of cayenne pepper. Serve with a garnish of fried croûtons—small dice of bread cooked in butter to a light golden colour.

MUSHROOMS EN BLANQUETTE

Make 1 pint of Velouté Sauce (see p. 68), but adding, at the same time as the veal stock, 1 medium-sized onion, stuck with 1 clove, a small carrot, a few sprigs of thyme, parsley, 1 small bayleaf. After 1 hour, strain the sauce, replace in another saucepan, and add 6 tablespoons of cream, mixed with the yolks of 2 eggs, and 2 teaspoons or more of lemon juice, according to taste. The sauce should be somewhat light. Now add ¾ lb. of button mushrooms and 12 pickling onions, blanched in boiling salted water for 5 minutes. Simmer for 15 minutes or longer, according to the size of the mushrooms, but do not let the sauce actually boil. When done, put on a hot dish, and sprinkle with a little chopped parsley.

MUSHROOMS À LA BORDELAISE

To every pound of mushrooms allow 4 ozs. of olive oil and 1 oz. of chopped shallots. Choose somewhat large mushrooms, peel them and remove the stalks. Put the oil in a deep frying pan and, when hot, add the mushrooms top downwards. After a few minutes turn them carefully and cook the other side. The time varies according to the size of the mushrooms—from 10 to 20 minutes should be sufficient if the oil is kept very hot. Just before serving, sprinkle with the chopped shallot and 1 teaspoon of chopped parsley.

MUSHROOMS EN BROCHETTE

Choose small or medium-sized mushrooms of equal size. Peel them and remove the stalks and thread them on silver or metal skewers alternately with chicken livers and thin pieces of lean bacon, cut the same size as the mushrooms. Season with salt and pepper, and either grill them or cook in hot butter or oil. If silver skewers are being used, serve on the skewers, but if ordinary kitchen ones are used, remove the skewer and serve on neat slices of hot buttered toast.

MUSHROOMS AND OYSTERS EN BROCHETTE

Prepare the mushrooms as in foregoing recipe, and put them on silver skewers, alternately with oysters, previously dipped in flour, seasoned with salt and pepper, then brushed over with yolk of egg and coated with fine white breadcrumbs. Either grill or fry in hot oil or butter. When done, add a dash of cayenne and a sprinkling of lemon juice, and serve very hot.

MUSHROOMS WITH BROWN BUTTER

Peel the mushrooms and remove the stalks. Toss lightly in butter in a frying pan, seasoning with salt and pepper. Cook for 10 to 12 minutes, according to the size of the mushrooms. When done, put on a hot dish and pour Brown Butter Sauce over them. This is made as follows: Put the amount of butter required in a small saucepan, and cook till it turns a darkish, nutty brown colour. Pour it over the mushrooms. In the same small saucepan, which is still very hot, put vinegar in the proportion of 1 tablespoon to every 2 ozs. of butter. Reduce rapidly and pour the vinegar over the mushrooms.

MUSHROOMS WITH BUTTER AND LEMON

This is an excellent way of cooking button mushrooms. Wash and dry them carefully, and trim them. If they are quite small it is not necessary to peel them. Put them in a saucepan with butter, allowing about 2½ to 3 ozs. of butter to every 1 lb. of mushrooms, the juice of 1 lemon, salt, pepper and a little grated nutmeg. Do not add any water. Cover the saucepan, put on a moderate fire, shake the saucepan occasionally and cook for about 8 to 10 minutes. Serve with a little of the butter poured over them.

MUSHROOMS À LA CATALANE (Hot)

Peel the mushrooms and, if large, divide them in quarters. Cook them in oil in the same manner as Mushrooms à la Bordelaise (see p. 28), and just before serving sprinkle them freely with fine brown breadcrumbs, 3 or 4 chopped cloves of garlic, 1 teaspoon of chopped parsley and season highly with salt and pepper.

MUSHROOMS À LA CATALANE (Cold)

To every pound of mushrooms, allow 3½ ozs. of olive oil, ½ a tumbler of white wine, 1 onion, 1 lemon, 4 cloves of garlic, mixed herbs, 1 teaspoon of chopped parsley, salt and pepper. Put the oil in a saucepan, add the chopped onion, and cook till soft, but without browning. Add the sliced garlic, the herbs and the white wine, season with salt and pepper, and let simmer for 5 minutes. Then add the lemon juice, and simmer for another 15 minutes. Now add the mushrooms, and simmer for 5 to 8 minutes. When done, put them in an earthenware terrine, with their marinade, and let stand till quite cold. Serve with a little of the strained marinade poured over them.

MUSHROOMS SOUS CLOCHE

Choose mushrooms of the same size and not too large. Peel carefully, having washed and dried them, and remove the stalks. Beat 2 tablespoons of butter to a cream with $\frac{1}{2}$ a tablespoon of lemon juice and a little salt, and spread in a round glass fireproof dish which has a lid. Cut a few rounds of bread about $\frac{1}{2}$ inch thick and about 2 inches in diameter, and put these in the dish. Over them place the mushrooms, piling them up in the shape of a cone. Season with salt and pepper, sprinkle with lemon juice, cover with 5 or 6 tablespoons of cream, and cover with the glass lid. Bake in a moderate oven for 25 to 30 minutes, adding more cream 10 minutes before serving, and just before serving flavour with 1 tablespoon of sherry or Madeira. Send to table with the lid on, and remove it only when once in the dining room. The delicious flavour of the mushrooms is thus fully preserved.

MUSHROOMS SOUS CLOCHE ON TOAST

Choose medium-sized mushrooms, peel them and remove the stalks. Put rounds of bread, lightly toasted, in a square or oblong shallow fireproof dish, side by side. The dish should be slightly buttered. On each round of toast, put a mushroom, with the stalk side upwards, garnish with a pat of Maître d'Hôtel butter (see Grilled Mushrooms, p. 23) and a small teaspoon of cream. Cover and cook in a moderate oven for about 20 to 25 minutes. Remove the lid just before serving.

MUSHROOMS WITH CREAM

Wash and peel the mushrooms and remove the stalks. If large, quarter or slice them, or leave whole if small. Toss in a little hot butter, with 1 tablespoon of chopped onion to every ½ lb. of mushrooms, the onions having been previously cooked in butter till quite soft, but without browning. Season with salt and pepper, and cook for 5 to 8 minutes, according to the size of the mushrooms. When nearly done, drain off the butter, and cover the mushrooms with boiling cream and simmer till reduced.

MUSHROOMS WITH CREAM À LA VALENTINOISE

Peel the mushrooms and remove the stalks. Melt a little butter in a deep frying pan, and when hot add the mushrooms, a few sprigs of parsley, chervil, tarragon, chopped chives, season with salt and pepper, and sprinkle with lemon juice. Toss the mushrooms and, when tender, remove the herbs, add 1 tablespoon of thick Tomato Sauce and 3 tablespoons of thick cream, to which the yolk of 1 egg has been added and well stirred in. Cook for a few minutes longer, pour into a hot dish and garnish with small croûtons of fried bread.

MUSHROOM CROQUETTES

Peel the mushrooms and remove the stalks. Cook either in butter and lemon juice (see p. 30) or in the way indicated for Mushrooms as a Garnish. Then chop finely both mushrooms and stalks, add chopped ham, allowing $\frac{1}{4}$ lb. of ham to each $\frac{1}{2}$ lb. of mushrooms, and mix with thick Béchamel Sauce (see p. 69), seasoned with a little lemon juice, and let stand till cold. The mixture should be sufficiently stiff to be easily handled and shaped. Shape into corks, roll in flour, coat with beaten yolk of egg, then with fine white breadcrumbs, and fry in a pan of deep and very hot oil. Cook to a light golden colour, drain, serve on a hot dish on a folded napkin and garnish with fried parsley. They can be served either plain or with Espagnole Sauce (see p. 65) or some other appropriate sauce, in a sauce-boat.

MUSHROOMS EN DAUBE

Put 4 tablespoons of olive oil in· a saucepan and, when hot, add 1 lb. of peeled mushrooms, either sliced or quartered. Season with salt and pepper, 1 or 2 cloves of garlic, sliced, 1 teaspoon of chopped parsley, and stir well. Then add ½ a tumbler of white wine, 2 tablespoons of lemon juice, and 4 or 5 fillets of anchovies in oil. Simmer for 15 to 20 minutes, and to serve, put the mushrooms on a hot dish, pour a little of the marinade over them and garnish with a few more fillets of anchovy in oil.

This dish is equally nice cold.

MUSHROOMS WITH EGGS

Choose large mushrooms, peel them and remove the stalk very close to the mushroom, so as to leave a slight hollow. Partially cook the mushrooms in a little hot oil or butter, seasoning them with salt and pepper. Have ready a deep frying pan with hot oil. When the mushrooms are partially cooked, remove them from the pan, and carefully break an egg on each. Slip the mushrooms, containing the eggs, very carefully in the frying pan of hot oil, and baste the eggs with a spoon with the hot oil till they are sufficiently set. Carefully remove from the oil with a perforated fish slice, and serve at once on very hot plates, with a sprinkling of chopped parsley. This dish is impossible to do unless the mushroom is of the right shape and size—it must be quite "cup-shaped" when the stalk has been removed.

MUSHROOMS À LA ESPAÑOLA

Wash medium-sized mushrooms, peel them and remove the stalks. Cook them in a little butter or oil, with a few tablespoons of good stock, seasoning with salt and pepper. When nearly done, strain away a little of the liquid in which they were cooked and add the following sauce: Dissolve 3 ozs. of butter in a small saucepan, bring to the boil, thicken with 1 teaspoon of flour, season with salt and pepper and add 1 to $1\frac{1}{2}$ ozs. of finely chopped sweet almonds, previously blanched and lightly browned in the oven. Simmer and stir for a few minutes, and mix with the mushrooms.

MUSHROOMS WITH ESPAGNOLE SAUCE

Cook the mushrooms in the manner indicated for Mushrooms as a Garnish (see p. 38), and add them to the Espagnole Sauce (see p. 65) a few minutes before serving.

MUSHROOMS AUX FINES HERBES

Peel the mushrooms and chop coarsely but evenly. Cook in hot butter, seasoning with salt and pepper. Just before serving, sprinkle them with a little chopped parsley, tarragon and chervil, and put on a hot dish. They can be garnished with croûtons of fried bread.

MUSHROOM FINGERS

Roll out some puff pastry on a floured board to a thickness of about $\frac{1}{4}$ inch and divide into strips about $1\frac{1}{2}$ inches wide and 3 inches long. On one side of the strips, place a little of the mixture for Mushroom Croquettes (see p. 33), fold the other side of the pastry over this, damping and pressing down the edges, so that they will not open when baked. They should have the appearance of small, narrow fingers. Brush over with beaten yolk of egg and brown in a brisk oven. These can be eaten either hot or cold.

Instead of being baked in the oven, they can also be fried in a deep pan of very hot oil.

MUSHROOM FRITTERS

Cook the mushrooms in the way described for Mushrooms as a Garnish (see p. 38). Drain and cut in $\frac{1}{2}$ inch pieces. Let stand till cold. Make the following frying batter: Put $\frac{1}{4}$ lb. of sifted flour in a salad bowl or an earthenware casserole, with a good pinch of salt. With the tips of the fingers push the flour to the sides of the bowl, equally all around, leaving a bare space or well in the middle. In this put 1 tablespoon of oil, the yolk of 1 egg, mixed, but not beaten.

Now start adding the flour gradually with a wooden spoon, drawing it towards the centre and mixing with the egg and oil. Then start adding, also very gradually, 1 gill of boiled milk. Mix till quite smooth. Let stand for 1 hour and, when about to use, add the white of egg, beaten to a stiff froth. Take 1 tablespoon at a time of the chopped mushrooms, dip in the batter and drop in a deep pan of very hot oil. Repeat the process till the mushrooms and batter are used up. Do not put too many fritters in at the same time or they will cling together. Cook to a light golden colour, turning carefully with a skimmer, so that both sides are equally coloured. Drain on a cloth or on a piece of blotting paper, and serve on a hot dish on a folded napkin, with a garnish of parsley.

MUSHROOMS AU GRATIN

Coat a fireproof dish with Duxelles Sauce (see p. 64) and over it place the mushrooms, previously cooked in the manner indicated for Mushrooms as a Garnish (see p. 38). Cover with another layer of Duxelles Sauce, sprinkle with breadcrumbs, moisten with melted butter, and brown in a quick oven.

MUSHROOMS AU GRATIN À LA RUSSE

Peel and remove the stalks from medium-sized mushrooms, season with salt and dip in flour. Cook them lightly in a few tablespoons of clarified butter, then place them in a fireproof dish, coat with Béchamel Sauce (see p. 69), to which 2 or 3 tablespoons of sour cream have been added, sprinkle with a little chopped fennel, breadcrumbs, and moisten with melted butter. Put in a brisk oven to brown.

MUSHROOMS AS A GARNISH

Choose the mushrooms as much as possible of the same size. Wash them rapidly in cold water. [As I have already said at the beginning of this book—and cannot say too often—mushrooms should never be allowed to stand in water.] Dry them thoroughly, remove the stalks and peel the mushrooms. To every $\frac{1}{2}$ lb. of mushrooms, allow 6 tablespoons of water, 1 heaped salt-spoon of salt, the juice of $\frac{1}{2}$ a lemon and 1 oz. of butter. Bring the salted water and the lemon juice to the boil, add the mushrooms and then the butter. Boil rapidly for 4 to 5 minutes, and the mushrooms are now ready for use. Remove from the fire, and leave them in the saucepan till required. They can then be drained and added to a sauce. They can be prepared in this manner the day before they are required, and kept in an earthenware terrine or casserole, with the liquid, and covered with buttered paper. To retain their full flavour, mushrooms should always be cooked in a small quantity of liquid and boiled rapidly. A common mistake is to add mushrooms to a sauce, or a stew, etc., and let them cook too long. The mushrooms are apt to become tough and to lose their flavour. When cooked in this manner, they can be added to the sauce, etc., only a few minutes before serving.

MUSHROOMS WITH SPAGHETTI

Have ready a large saucepan of boiling salted water—the water must be plentiful and on the full boil. Put in ½ lb. of spaghetti, *unbroken*. It is a common mistake to break up these Italian pastes, such as spaghetti and macaroni, in short lengths. The flavour is very much improved when they are left whole. As soon as one end is immersed in the boiling water, it collapses and the other end slips of itself into the saucepan. If the spaghetti is quite thin, it will be sufficiently cooked in 5 or 6 minutes. It must be soft, but not sodden. Remove from the fire and quickly drain on a collander. Melt 2 ozs. of butter in a frying pan, add ½ lb. of quartered tomatoes and cook till soft. Then add the spaghetti, mix with the tomatoes, season with salt and pepper, and cook for 10 minutes, stirring occasionally with a wooden spoon. Add 4 tablespoons of grated Parmesan cheese. Now put the contents of the pan in a well-buttered china fireproof dish—a fluted soufflé dish is best—sprinkle with more Parmesan cheese, pour a little melted butter over the whole,

and put in a moderate oven for 25 minutes. Ten
minutes before serving, mix in ½ lb. of mushrooms,
halved or quartered, according to their size, and
previously cooked as in the foregoing recipe.
Serve in the same dish.

MUSHROOMS WITH MADEIRA

Choose 1 lb. of medium-sized mushrooms,
wash and peel them and remove the stalks. Melt
2 ozs. of butter in a saucepan and add 1 oz. of
flour, working to a smooth paste, letting it brown
lightly. Then add gradually ½ pint of boiling
stock, stirring well, a sprig or two of parsley
and thyme, 1 small bayleaf, and season with a
little salt and pepper. Put in the mushrooms and
simmer for 30 to 35 minutes, according to the
size of the mushrooms. A few minutes before
serving, add 1 gill of Madeira. Put on a hot dish
and garnish with croûtons of fried bread.

MUSHROOMS MARINATED

Cook 1 lb. of small button mushrooms as for a
Garnish (see p. 38). Put ½ pint of vinegar in a
saucepan with 6 tablespoons of olive oil, 1 finely
chopped clove of garlic, a sprig or two of thyme,
1 bayleaf, a few coriander seeds, coarse salt,
peppercorns, a few sprigs of fennel and parsley.
Bring to the boil and simmer for 5 minutes. Put
the mushrooms in an earthenware vessel, and

pour the boiling marinade over them. Cover and let stand till quite cold.

MUSHROOMS MARINATED À LA RUSSE

Cook small mushrooms as for a Garnish (see p. 38). Drain and, when cold, pack them closely in jars having air-tight lids, with 1 or 2 cloves of garlic, 2 or 3 bayleaves, a few sprigs of fennel, peppercorns and salt. Cover with cold boiled vinegar, pour a little olive oil on the top, and screw on the lid. These are popular as a winter salad, with a French salad dressing, consisting of 2 tablespoons of olive oil to 1 tablespoon of vinegar —preferably wine vinegar—and a seasoning of salt and pepper.

MUSHROOMS À LA MORNAY

Add 1 lb. of small mushrooms, previously cooked as for a Garnish (see p. 38), to 1 pint of Mornay Sauce (see p. 70) a few minutes before serving.

MUSHROOMS À LA NAPOLITAINE

Prepare and cook the mushrooms as for a Garnish (see p. 38). Drain, and brown lightly in oil or butter in a sauté pan, with 1 or 2 cloves of garlic and $\frac{1}{2}$ lb. of sliced tomatoes to every pound of mushrooms, seasoning with salt and pepper.

MUSHROOMS WITH NORMANDE SAUCE

Cook 1 lb. of small mushrooms as for a Garnish (see p. 38). Make a Sauce Normande in the following way: Melt 1 oz. of butter in a saucepan and, when very hot, add 1 finely chopped onion and brown it lightly. Then add 2 ozs. of butter and work to a smooth paste with 1 oz. of flour. Dilute gradually with ½ pint, or a little over, of white wine or cider, season with salt, pepper and a little nutmeg, and 5 minutes before serving stir in 6 tablespoons of cream and 2 teaspoons of lemon juice. Warm up the mushrooms in the sauce.

MUSHROOM OMELET

To every 3 eggs used in making an omelet, allow 2 ozs. of chopped mushrooms and 6 thin slices of mushroom as a garnish (see p. 38). Chop the mushrooms and cook them for a few minutes in butter, then add to the eggs already beaten for the making of the omelet. Make the omelet in the usual way, fold, slip it on to a hot dish and garnish with slices of mushroom, lightly cooked in butter, and season with salt and pepper.

MUSHROOMS IN THE OVEN

This is a novel way of cooking mushrooms, but the greatest care should be exercised as they are apt to burn. The mushrooms are washed, well dried, their stalks removed, but they are not peeled. Put them on a hot pan without any liquid and cook in a slow oven till tender. The pan should be frequently shaken. They are then placed on a hot dish, and melted butter, seasoned with salt and pepper, is poured over them. They must be done quite slowly, and should not be in the slightest way shrivelled.

MUSHROOM AND OYSTER SAVOURY

Choose large mushrooms as much as possible of the same size. Peel them, remove the stalks, and cook for 3 or 4 minutes only as for Garnish (see p. 38). Drain thoroughly, and place in a buttered fireproof dish top downwards. On each put an oyster, wrapped in a thin rasher of lean bacon, and put in a fairly brisk oven. When the bacon is done, remove the dish from the oven, put each mushroom on a large round of toasted bread and sprinkle the whole with a little lemon juice. Serve very hot.

MUSHROOM PANCAKES

Chop the mushrooms and cook in a little butter, seasoning with salt and pepper. Mix with equal parts of light pancake batter, unsweetened and seasoned with salt. Make the pancakes in the ordinary way, but keeping them very thin. Fold, put on a hot dish and serve with quartered lemons.

MUSHROOMS EN PAPILLOTES

Choose medium-sized button mushrooms for this dish. Cook them as for a Garnish (see p. 38) and drain. Put 3 or 4 mushrooms on silver skewers, coat with a layer of very thick Duxelles Sauce (see p. 64) and place each skewer on a paper papillote prepared as follows: Get some plain foolscap paper and cut in the shape of a large heart, the centre of the heart being where the paper is folded. Cut out neatly, then open the sheet, lay it flat on a table and paint all over with a little olive oil. Place the skewer with the mushrooms on one side of the paper, in a slightly slanting position, fold the other side of the paper over it, and now fold the edges over, crinkling them as you go on, so that the case thus formed will not come undone. Put the papillotes on a baking tin, and place in a moderate oven till the paper begins to brown. Serve in the paper cases.

MUSHROOMS WITH PAPRIKA

Chop 2 or 3 onions finely and fry in a little lard till brown. Then add 12 ozs. of small peeled mushrooms, season with salt and 1 tablespoon of paprika, and add sufficient warm water barely to cover the mushrooms. Cover the saucepan and simmer very gently till the mushrooms are tender and the water has completely evaporated. Just before serving, stir in 2 tablespoons of sour cream.

MUSHROOM PÂTÉ OR PIE

Line a deep fireproof dish or a pie dish with slices of ham, over this place mushrooms, previously lightly cooked in butter, sprinkle with chopped onion, chopped parsley and mixed herbs, seasoning with salt and pepper, and continue filling the dish in alternate layers, the top layer being ham. Moisten with stock or Espagnole Sauce (see p. 65), cover with a lid of either puff pastry or short crust, leaving a small opening in the centre, and decorate the pie with pastry leaves, etc. Brush over with beaten yolk of egg, and bake in a moderate oven for $\frac{3}{4}$ hour to 1 hour, according to the size of the pie. A few minutes before serving pour in a little hot stock or Espagnole Sauce, cover the opening with pastry, and replace in the oven.

MUSHROOM PÂTÉS (Small)

Have ready a few pâtés cases of puff pastry. Choose small button mushrooms and cook them as for a Garnish (see p. 38). Put 2 or 3 of them in each pâté case, moisten with a little thick Duxelles, or Béchamel, or Mornay Sauce (see pp. 64, 69 or 70) according to taste, cover with the pastry lid and put in the oven for 10 minutes till thoroughly hot.

MUSHROOM PIROSHKI

Cook 1 lb. of small mushrooms as for a Garnish (see p. 38), drain and cut them in half. Put a thin layer of puff pastry on a baking tin or on a round baking plate, cover with the mushrooms mixed with 1 or 2 finely chopped hardboiled eggs, and moisten with a little Béchamel Sauce (see p. 69). Cover with a thin layer of puff pastry, damping and pressing down the edges, brush the whole with beaten yolk of egg and bake for $\frac{1}{2}$ hour in a moderate oven, till the pastry has risen and is a light golden colour.

MUSHROOMS À LA POULETTE

See Poulette Sauce (p. 66). Instead of adding only 2 or 3 mushrooms to the sauce, cook 1 lb. of small mushrooms, previously peeled, in the sauce for 20 minutes.

MUSHROOMS À LA PROVENÇALE

Choose 1 lb. of medium-sized mushrooms, wash them, peel and remove the stalks. Put them in a deep dish and sprinkle freely with olive oil, salt, peppercorns and a little chopped garlic. Let them stand for 1 hour, turning occasionally. Then toss or *sauté* them in a deep frying pan in hot oil, till they are lightly browned, and, just before serving, add a sprinkling of parsley, about 12 croûtons of fried bread and the juice of 1 lemon.

MUSHROOM PULAO

Put 2 ozs. of butter in a saucepan and, when hot, fry 2 small sliced onions in it to a golden brown. Then add ½ lb. of rice, and 6 ozs. of butter, and cook till the rice has absorbed most of the butter, stirring frequently. Season with salt and peppercorns. Then add 2 tablespoons of stoned almonds, a few small sticks of cinnamon, a few cardamon seeds, 1 or 2 bayleaves, and barely cover with boiling water. Put the lid on the saucepan and simmer very gently till the rice is tender. Remove the rice from the saucepan, mix with ¾ lb. of small mushrooms, previously cooked as for a Garnish, sprinkle the whole with a little saffron, and put in a moderate oven for a few minutes, so that the moisture will evaporate from the rice.

MUSHROOM QUENELLES

Beat the yolks of 2 eggs in a basin with the equivalent in size of a small egg of butter. When quite creamy, add gradually and alternately the whites of eggs beaten to a stiff froth and very fine brown breadcrumbs, mixed with equal parts of finely chopped cooked mushrooms, and season with salt and pepper. When the mixture is sufficiently stiff to be handled, shape into very small balls, and poach in boiling salted water for 8 to 10 minutes. Drain thoroughly. These are excellent as a garnish for soups, or stews, etc., or they can be served separately, mixed with some kind of sauce, such as Espagnole, Béchamel, etc.

MUSHROOM RAGOÛT À LA SAVOYARDE

Wash and peel 1 lb. of small mushrooms. Cook them as for a Garnish (see p. 38), but keep them quite firm. Drain, and put in a deep frying pan with a little butter, the juice of 1 lemon, and season highly with salt and pepper. In a small saucepan mix 1½ ozs. of butter with 1 oz. of flour and stir to a smooth paste with a wooden spoon, over a very slow fire, till lightly brown. Then dilute gradually with a little over ½ pint of white wine, and, when the sauce is quite smooth, pour it over the mushrooms, mix well and simmer for another 10 minutes.

MUSHROOMS WITH RISOTTO

Cook 1 small chopped onion to a light golden brown in 2 ozs. of butter in a saucepan. Add 6 ozs. of sliced mushrooms, and cook for another 5 minutes over a slow fire. Then add 1 lb. of rice (preferably Italian rice), 2 pints of boiling chicken broth or good stock, season highly with salt and pepper, stir well, and simmer gently for 30 minutes, till the rice has absorbed the stock. Remove from the fire, and mix with 2 ozs. of melted butter and 6 6zs. of grated Parmesan cheese.

MUSHROOM ROLLS

This is an extremely tempting way of serving mushrooms which have been either cooked in a little butter, with a seasoning of lemon juice, salt and pepper, or grilled, and it makes an excellent and substantial breakfast or luncheon dish. Cut the top from a few round French dinner rolls—the ones which have a nice crisp crust. Scoop out the soft part of the roll—this bread need not be wasted; it can be used for stuffings, for making breadcrumbs, etc. Moisten the inside of the roll with a little milk and melted butter, and put in the oven till piping hot. Fill each roll with the cooked mushrooms and moisten with a little of the butter in which they were cooked. Serve very hot and on very hot plates.

The rolls are even crisper and nicer if, instead of being put in the oven, they are put in a deep frying pan in very hot oil, and basted with the hot oil for a few minutes and drained.

MUSHROOMS ROSSINI

See Mushrooms with Cream (p. 32). Proceed in exactly the same manner, but add a few sliced truffles.

MUSHROOM SALAD

The best mushrooms for a salad are the medium-sized button mushrooms. If large mushrooms are used they should be quartered. Peel the mushrooms and remove the stalks. Cook as for Mushrooms as a Garnish (see p. 38). Drain thoroughly, put in a salad bowl and mix with a plain French salad dressing, made with 2 tablespoons of oil to 1 of vinegar, and season highly with salt and black pepper.

MUSHROOMS SAUTÉS WITH PARSLEY

Peel the mushrooms, remove the stalks, and either leave whole or quartered or slice them, according to their size. Toss them in hot butter for 10 to 12 minutes, or less if small, season with salt and pepper, and just before serving add a good squeeze of lemon juice and sprinkle freely with finely chopped parsley.

MUSHROOMS WITH WHITE WINE

Prepare the mushrooms as in the foregoing recipe and toss in hot butter. Sprinkle with a little flour, mix well and let the flour brown. Then add 4 tablespoons of white wine to every $\frac{1}{2}$ lb. of mushrooms, mix thoroughly and cook for another 5 to 8 minutes.

MUSHROOMS WITH SAUERKRAUT

Wash 2 lbs. of sauerkraut thoroughly in cold water, drain, and put in a saucepan or earthenware casserole with $\frac{1}{2}$ pint of sour cream, $\frac{3}{4}$ lb. of dried mushrooms (see p. 84), previously soaked and

cooked as for a Garnish (see p. 38) and chopped.
Cover and simmer on a slow fire or in the oven for
about 40 to 60 minutes, till the sauerkraut is
quite tender. This dish is often served in Russia
as a zakouska or hors d'œuvre.

MUSHROOMS AND SHEEP'S BRAIN À LA POULETTE

Soak the sheep's brain in cold water for at least
2 hours, changing the water frequently. Carefully
remove the skin and fibres and soak once more in
warm water for about ½ hour. Drain and put in a
saucepan and cover with cold water. Add salt,
bring to the boil and simmer for 3 or 4 minutes.
Drain thoroughly. When cold, cut into slices,
and cook for a few minutes in a Poulette Sauce
with Mushrooms (see Mushrooms à la Poulette,
p. 66).

MUSHROOMS IN SHELLS

Chop the mushrooms coarsely, having previously cooked them as for a Garnish (see p. 38).
Half fill a few buttered scallop shells with them.
Spread over each a tablespoon of well-beaten egg,
mixed with a little chopped shallot and anchovy,
and put in a brisk oven till the egg is cooked and
serve at once.

MUSHROOMS WITH SOUBISE SAUCE

Cook 1 lb. of peeled mushrooms as for a Garnish (see p. 38). Peel 1 lb. of onions and chop them very finely. Blanch in boiling salted water for 10 minutes, drain thoroughly, and simmer in a little butter till quite soft, but without browning. Then add 1 pint of Béchamel Sauce (see p. 69), season with salt, pepper and a pinch of sugar, and simmer very gently for $\frac{1}{2}$ hour. Rub through a sieve, replace the sauce in a saucepan, put on a slow fire and, when hot, but not boiling, stir in 2 ozs. of butter, divided in small pieces, and 4 tablespoons of cream. The sauce should be very white and creamy. Add the cooked mushrooms about 5 minutes before serving, so that they are thoroughly hot, but do not boil.

MUSHROOM SOUFFLÉ

Cook $\frac{3}{4}$ lb. of mushrooms as for a Garnish (see p. 38) but cooking them a little longer than indicated, so that they are soft. Drain thoroughly, chop finely and pound in a mortar or put through a mincer. Mix with 4 tablespoons of cold Béchamel Sauce, rub through a sieve and warm in a saucepan over a slow fire, but without boiling. Add 1 oz. of butter, the yolks of 3 eggs, and mix thoroughly. Remove from the fire and when nearly cold, add the whites of 4 eggs beaten to a stiff froth. Pour the mixture into a buttered soufflé dish, filling it only $\frac{3}{4}$ full, and put in a fairly brisk oven at first. When the soufflé begins to rise, lower the temperature. Bake for 20 to 25 minutes and serve at once.

MUSHROOM SOUFFLÉ (Cold)

Cook $\frac{1}{2}$ lb. of mushrooms as for a Garnish (see p. 38), but cooking them for a few minutes longer, so that they are soft. Drain thoroughly, chop and pound them in a mortar with $\frac{1}{4}$ lb. of lean ham. Add gradually 3 tablespoons of cold Béchamel Sauce (see p. 69), mix thoroughly and rub the whole through a sieve. Mix very gradually with $\frac{1}{2}$ pint of stiffly whipped cream, to which $\frac{1}{2}$ oz. of dissolved gelatine has been added. Beat till very light and turn into small fluted paper cases, or if preferred into a mould and stand in a cold place till set. If put in a mould, before turning out, dip the mould in warm water for a few seconds, dry it and the soufflé will come out easily.

MUSHROOMS AND SWEETBREAD

Prepare and blanch the sweetbread in the following manner: Soak the sweetbread in cold water for at least 4 hours, renewing the water every time it becomes tinted with blood. If this is not done, the inside of the sweetbread will always remain pink, even after cooking, and sweetbread should always be quite white and free from all traces of blood before being cooked. Put the sweetbread in a saucepan and cover with cold water. Bring to the boil and boil for exactly 2 minutes. This makes the sweetbread firm and easier to handle. Drain and trim the sweetbread, being careful however, not to pierce the thin membrane which holds it together. Lay the sweetbread on a cloth, fold the cloth over it, cover with a board and put a 2 lb. weight over it. Let stand for 1 hour.

Put a layer of Duxelles Sauce (see p. 64) in a shallow fireproof dish, and over it put the sliced sweetbread. Between each slice put a medium-sized, peeled mushroom. Cover with Duxelles Sauce, sprinkle with breadcrumbs, moisten with a little melted butter, and put in a moderate oven for 30 to 35 minutes, till the sweetbread is quite tender. Serve in the same dish.

MUSHROOM TARTLETS

Line tartlet tins with either puff pastry or short crust, and fill with the same mixture as for Flan of Mushrooms (see p. 22). The tartlets can also be covered with very thin bands of pastry, forming a trellis, in the same way as the Flan.

MUSHROOMS ON TOAST

These can be prepared in various ways. The mushrooms can either be grilled (see recipes for Grilled Mushrooms, p. 23), and served on hot buttered toast, or they can be tossed in butter, and served in the same way, or cooked as for a Garnish (see p. 38) and mixed with some appropriate sauce (see Sauces, pp. 63-70). The manner of serving mushrooms on toast can be varied almost indefinitely, according to individual taste.

MUSHROOMS WITH TOMATO PURÉE

Quarter $1\frac{1}{2}$ lbs. of tomatoes, and put them in a saucepan with $1\frac{1}{2}$ ozs. of butter, a sprig of rosemary and simmer over a slow fire for 1 to $1\frac{1}{2}$ hours, stirring occasionally with a wooden spoon, and seasoning with salt, pepper and a pinch of sugar. Rub through a sieve and replace in a saucepan, on a slow fire, to get thoroughly hot. Add the finely chopped mushroom stalks, previously cooked for a few minutes in butter. Pour the Tomato Sauce into a shallow glass fireproof dish, over it place somewhat large mushrooms, previously cooked as for a Garnish (see p. 38), and with the inner side uppermost. On each mushroom put a thin slice of truffle and a very small pat of butter, and put in a brisk oven for 5 to 8 minutes. Sprinkle with finely chopped parsley, and serve in the same dish.

MUSHROOMS À LA TOSCANA

Choose 1 lb. of medium-sized mushrooms, peel them and remove the stalks. Put 3 tablespoons of olive oil in a saucepan and, when hot, put in the mushrooms and cook till slightly browned. Then barely cover with Tomato Purée made as in the previous recipe, add 2 or 3 sprigs of marjoram and 2 or 3 cloves of garlic. Simmer very gently for 25 to 30 minutes.

PANCAKES STUFFED WITH MUSHROOMS

Make light and thin pancakes in the ordinary way, but unsweetened, and with a good pinch of salt added to the batter. Before folding, put in 1 tablespoon of chopped mushrooms, well browned in butter and seasoned with salt, pepper and a little lemon juice. Serve very hot, with quartered lemons.

MUSHROOM PURÉE

Cook 1 lb. of mushrooms as for a Garnish (see p. 38), rub them through a sieve, and mix with a sufficient quantity of thick Béchamel Sauce to give the purée the right consistency.

MUSHROOM PURÉE (Alternative Version)

Chop 1 lb. of uncooked mushrooms and rub them through a sieve. Put this into a saucepan with 1 oz. of butter and stir over a quick fire till all the moisture has evaporated. Then add 1 gill of thick Béchamel Sauce (see p. 69) and stir well, and next add 3 tablespoons of cream.

Season with salt, pepper and a little grated nut-meg. Remove from the fire and stir in 2 ozs. of butter, divided in small pieces.

STEWED MUSHROOMS

Cook the mushrooms as for a Garnish (see p. 38), but using either cream or milk instead of water. Put the mushrooms in the cream or milk, flavoured with a little lemon juice, and add the butter. Simmer for 12 to 15 minutes. Serve with the cream or milk poured over them.

STEWED MUSHROOMS IN THE CHINESE WAY

This dish is made with dried mushrooms. Soak 6 ozs. of mushrooms in hot water for 15 minutes, drain and remove the stalks. Crush 2 cloves of garlic with the blade of a knife and put in a hot oiled pan, cook for a few seconds and remove the garlic from the pan. Put the mushrooms in the same pan and cook for 10 minutes. Now put the mushrooms in a saucepan with a quarter more than sufficient stock to cover, add 1 small piece of ginger, crushed with a knife, bring to the boil and simmer for 6 hours. Serve with Chinese Shoyu Sauce. If the latter is not obtainable, the Japanese Shoyu Sauce, which is now on the market in England, can be used.

STUFFED MUSHROOMS

Choose somewhat large mushrooms of equal size. Remove the stalks and, with a sharp knife, scoop out a little hollow from where the stalks were removed. Do not peel the mushrooms. Put them in a fireproof dish, season with salt and pepper, sprinkle freely with oil and cook in a fairly quick oven for a few minutes, till tender, and till their moisture has evaporated. Fill the hollow in each mushroom with thick Duxelles Sauce (see p. 64), sprinkle with breadcrumbs, moisten with a little melted butter, and brown in a brisk oven.

MUSHROOMS STUFFED WITH BACON

Choose large or medium-sized mushrooms, peel them and remove the stalks. Chop the stalks finely and mix with equal parts of chopped bacon, lean and fat. Cook both in a little butter, sprinkle with lemon juice and bind with the yolks of 1 or 2 eggs. Cook the mushrooms as for a Garnish, but keeping them quite firm. Drain, cover the stalk-side of the mushrooms with a layer of the stuffing, sprinkle with breadcrumbs, add a dash of cayenne and put in a fireproof dish, with a little butter and a few tablespoons of stock. Cook in a moderate oven for 10 to 15 minutes, basting frequently. Serve on a hot dish, with a little of the melted butter and stock.

MUSHROOMS STUFFED A LA BORDELAISE

Choose somewhat large mushrooms, peel them and remove the stalks. Chop these finely, mix with a little chopped shallot, parsley and stale breadcrumbs. Cook in butter and 2 or 3 tablespoons of white wine, seasoning with salt, pepper and a little lemon juice. Season the mushrooms with salt and pepper, brush over with a little olive oil and grill them, or toss them in butter. When they are nearly done, cover the stalk side of each with the prepared stuffing, sprinkle with breadcrumbs and finish cooking in a buttered fireproof dish in the oven.

MUSHROOMS STUFFED WITH CHICKEN LIVERS

Proceed as in the previous recipe, but make the stuffing with equal parts of chopped chicken livers and chopped mushroom stalks, previously cooked in butter, with a little chopped shallot and parsley.

MUSHROOMS STUFFED WITH FISH

Proceed as in the foregoing recipes, but mix chopped cooked fish with the chopped cooked mushroom stalks. Warm both up in either a thick Duxelles Sauce (see p. 64) or a thick Béchamel Sauce. Pack the stuffed mushrooms somewhat closely in a buttered fireproof dish, sprinkle with breadcrumbs and finish cooking in a somewhat brisk oven.

STUFFED MUSHROOMS À LA LIMOUSINE

Peel and remove the stalks from large or medium-sized mushrooms. Chop finely equal parts of veal and fresh pork, and lightly brown in butter or oil, with 1 or 2 cloves of chopped garlic, chopped parsley, thyme and marjoram, with a seasoning of salt and pepper. When nearly done, bind with 1 or 2 eggs, and put a layer on each mushroom. Pack the mushrooms closely in an earthenware dish, well buttered, dot with pats of butter, cover with buttered or oiled paper and put in a moderate oven for 25 to 30 minutes. Serve in the same dish.

STUFFED MUSHROOMS À LA PÉRIGORD

Peel and remove the stalks from large or medium-sized mushrooms. Chop the stalks and mix with equal parts of bread, previously soaked in milk and squeezed, a quarter of the quantity of gammon, 1 chopped clove of garlic and a little parsley. Season with salt and pepper. Butter an earthenware or a fireproof dish, put in the mushrooms, top downwards, cover each with a layer of the stuffing, and put in a moderate oven. After

10 minutes, add a gill or ½ pint of thin Tomato purée—the quantity varies according to the quantity of mushrooms—and finish cooking. To serve, put the stuffed mushrooms on a hot dish and pour the sauce over them.

STUFFED MUSHROOMS À LA POLONAISE

Trim 2½ lbs. of mushrooms, peel them and remove the stalks. Chop these and mix with 1 chopped chicken or duck liver, 3 ozs. of pickled ox tongue, ½ an onion, and brown all these mixed ingredients in butter, seasoning with salt, pepper, paprika and lemon juice. When nearly done, bind with an egg. Cook the mushrooms as for a Garnish (see p. 38), keeping them quite firm. Drain, put in a buttered pan or fireproof dish, cover each with a layer of prepared stuffing, and bake in a moderate oven for 25 to 30 minutes, basting with butter.

MUSHROOMS STUFFED WITH TRUFFLES

Chop 3 or 4 large truffles coarsely (bottled or tinned truffles, which are already cooked) and put in a saucepan with a little butter and 2 or 3 teaspoons of brandy. Mix with a little cream, season with salt and pepper and simmer for a few minutes, till the cream begins to thicken. Peel the mushrooms and remove the stalks, and cook as for a Garnish (see p. 38). Drain thoroughly, put in a fireproof dish, with a little butter, somewhat closely packed, and cover each with a layer of the truffle mixture.

MUSHROOMS STUFFED WITH TUNNY FISH

Choose medium-sized mushrooms, peel them and remove the stalks. Cook as for a Garnish (see p. 38), drain thoroughly and let stand till cold. Then cover each mushroom with a layer of tunny fish, previously pounded in a mortar to a paste—tunny fish in oil is used for this—and dress with a salad dressing of 2 tablespoons of oil to 1 of vinegar, with a little salt and pepper.

Sauces with Mushrooms

ALLEMANDE SAUCE

Ingredients: 1½ pints of white veal stock, 3½ ozs. of butter, 1 oz. of flour, 3 ozs. of mushrooms or mushroom peelings, a few sprigs of parsley, the yolks of 4 eggs, salt, pepper and a little grated nutmeg.

Method: A thick saucepan should be used for making this sauce. Melt 1½ ozs. of butter and stir in the flour, working to a smooth paste. Then dilute gradually with the hot stock, add the chopped mushrooms, the parsley, and season with salt and pepper. Simmer very gently for 1 hour. Strain through a wire sieve, and replace in the saucepan, which should have been well rinsed. Mix the yolks of 4 eggs in a basin and moisten gradually with a few tablespoons of the hot liquid, then add them to the sauce, bring to the boil on a quick fire, and stir until the sauce is reduced to ½ pint. Strain once more through a wire sieve, add 2 ozs. of butter, divided in small pieces, and use as required.

CHASSEUR SAUCE

Put ½ oz. of butter in a saucepan and, when melted, add the same quantity of flour. Stir to a smooth paste, letting the mixture brown, and add gradually ½ pint of hot stock. Stir in 1½ tablespoons of thick tomato sauce, season with salt and pepper, and simmer for 10 to 12 minutes, without covering the saucepan. Meanwhile, chop 4 large mushrooms, and cook them in a little oil till lightly browned, add 2 chopped shallots, and cook together for 6 or 7 minutes longer. Drain off the oil, add 6 tablespoons of white wine, and let reduce by half. Now pour the prepared sauce over the mushrooms, stir well, and simmer for 6 or 7 minutes longer. Just before serving add 1 teaspoon of tarragon and chervil, a small lump of butter, remove from the fire and add a sprinkling of parsley.

DUXELLES SAUCE

Put 2 tablespoons of oil and 1 teaspoon of butter in a small thick saucepan. When hot, add 1 dessertspoon of chopped onion and 1 chopped shallot, and cook to a light golden colour, but without browning. Now add 3 ozs. of finely chopped mushrooms, season with salt, pepper and a little nutmeg. Stir for 5 to 6 minutes, add 6 tablespoons of white wine, 1 pint of good stock, 1 tablespoon of tomato purée and thicken with $\frac{1}{2}$ oz. of butter worked with the same quantity of flour. Stir, and simmer gently for 15 to 20 minutes. Just before serving, add 1 oz. of butter, divided in small pieces, and 1 teaspoon of chopped parsley.

ESPAGNOLE SAUCE

Ingredients: 2½ pints of good strong stock, 1 gill of white wine, 3 tablespoons of tomato purée, 3½ ozs. of lean bacon, 3½ ozs. of carrots, 3½ ozs. of onions, 1½ ozs. of mushrooms or mushroom peelings, 3 or 4 sprigs of parsley, a little thyme, 1 small bayleaf, 2 ozs. of flour, 3½ ozs. of butter.

Method: Cut the bacon, vegetables and mushrooms into small dice. Use a thick saucepan, put it on a slow fire and melt the butter. When the butter is just hot, add the bacon, vegetables and herbs, and cook very slowly till slightly browned. Do not cover the saucepan, and stir the vegetables and bacon occasionally with a wooden spoon so that they will be equally browned. Now sprinkle in the flour and mix thoroughly. Let all cook till brown, which will take from 15 to 20 minutes. Then add gradually the white wine and the hot stock, stirring continuously. Add the tomato purée, bring to the boil, add the mushrooms, and let simmer gently for 1 hour without covering the saucepan. Skim carefully as the grease rises to the surface. Then strain the sauce into another saucepan, put on a slow fire, bring to the boil, and skim until all the scum has come to the surface. This sauce should be absolutely free from any trace of grease.

MUSHROOM SAUCE (Brown)

Wash and peel $\frac{1}{4}$ lb. of mushrooms, and chop coarsely both mushrooms and stalks. Brown both lightly in a little butter, drain and add to 1 pint of hot Espagnole Sauce (see preceding recipe), and simmer for 20 minutes.

MUSHROOM SAUCE (White)

Proceed as in foregoing recipe, but using $\frac{1}{4}$ lb. of small button mushrooms and cooking them in 1 pint of Béchamel Sauce (see p. 69) for 20 minutes.

MUSHROOM SAUCE WITH CREAM

Melt $\frac{1}{4}$ lb. of butter in a small thick saucepan over a slow fire and, when hot, add $\frac{1}{2}$ pint of cream, and season with salt and pepper. Stir continuously with a wooden spoon for 10 minutes but without letting the sauce boil. A few minutes before serving add $\frac{1}{4}$ lb. of small button mushrooms, previously cooked as for a Garnish (see p. 38).

POULETTE SAUCE

Peel and wash 3 or 4 medium-sized mushrooms, quarter them and cook in a little butter, seasoning with salt, pepper and a dash of lemon juice. Cook till tender but without browning, then add 1 pint of Allemande Sauce (see p. 63), 1 tablespoon of lemon juice, stir well and simmer for a few minutes.

PROVENÇALE SAUCE WITH MUSHROOMS

Peel and chop 12 large and ripe tomatoes. Put them in a saucepan with 1 gill of olive oil, 1 clove of garlic, well crushed with the blade of a knife, 1 teaspoon of chopped parsley, and season with salt, pepper and a little sugar. Cover the saucepan and simmer gently for about ¾ of an hour. Ten minutes before serving add 2 or 3 medium-sized mushrooms, chopped, and previously cooked lightly in a little oil.

SAUCE À LA PURÉE DE CHAMPIGNONS

Chop 1 lb. of mushrooms, preferably white mushrooms, and rub them through a sieve. Put ½ a large onion, 1 medium-sized carrot, 1 small piece of turnip, all sliced, into a saucepan with 1 oz. of butter, ½ a bayleaf, a sprig of parsley, and 1 oz. of lean uncooked ham, chopped. Simmer over a slow fire till the vegetables are tender, but without browning. Add the sieved mushrooms, 8 tablespoons of Béchamel Sauce (see p. 69), season with salt, a pinch of sugar, and simmer for 10 minutes. Rub all through a sieve, replace in a saucepan, add 4 tablespoons of cream, and stir for a few minutes over a slow fire.

VELOUTÉ SAUCE

Ingredients: 1 pint of veal or chicken stock, 1 oz. of butter, just under 1 oz. of flour, 2 ozs. of mushroom peelings and stalks, 2 or 3 sprigs of parsley, salt and pepper.

Method: Melt the butter in a thick saucepan and stir in the flour. Work till smooth, but without browning. Then add the hot stock gradually, whipping the sauce unceasingly with a whisk, bring to the boil and skim carefully. Add the finely chopped mushroom stalks and peelings, the parsley, and season with salt and pepper. Simmer gently for 1 hour, removing every particle of grease, and just before serving strain through a wire sieve.

WOW-WOW SAUCE
(Old English, eighteenth century)

"Chop some parsley leaves very finely, quarter 2 or 3 pickled cucumbers or walnuts, divide them into small squares, and set them by ready; put into a saucepan a bit of butter as big as an egg; when it is melted, stir to it a tablespoon of fine flour, and about half a pint of the broth in which the beef was boiled; add a tablespoon of vinegar, the like quantity of mushroom ketchup or Port wine, or both, and a teaspoon of made mustard; let it simmer together till it is as thick as you wish it; put in parsley and pickles to get warm" —and use as required.

Sauces Mentioned in Recipes

BÉCHAMEL SAUCE

Ingredients: 1½ ozs. of onions, 1½ ozs. of carrots, 1½ ozs. of uncooked ham or gammon, or 2½ ozs. of veal, 2½ ozs. of butter, 1½ ozs. of flour, 1½ pints of either veal stock or milk, a bouquet of mixed herbs, salt, pepper and a little grated nutmeg.

Method: Chop the carrots and onions and cut the veal or ham in small dice. Put them in a saucepan with 1 oz. of butter, and simmer for 10 to 15 minutes, but without browning. Melt 1½ ozs. of butter in another small saucepan and work with the flour to a smooth paste, but without browning. Stir in the boiling stock or milk gradually. Now drain the butter from the vegetables and meat, and add the latter to the sauce, with the herb bouquet and a seasoning of salt, pepper and a little nutmeg. Bring to the boil, and simmer very gently for ¾ of an hour to 1 hour. When done, strain through a wire sieve into another small saucepan and stir in a small piece of butter. The sauce is now ready for use. It should be quite creamy.

MORNAY SAUCE

To every pint of Béchamel Sauce add 1 oz. of finely-grated Gruyère cheese and the same quantity of finely-grated Parmesan cheese. Stir over the fire till the cheese has melted and, just before serving, add 1 oz. of butter, divided in small pieces.

Mushroom Garnishes and Stuffings

DUXELLES (Dry)

This can be used for stuffings, garnishes, sauces, etc. Melt 1 oz. of butter with the same quantity of oil, in a saucepan, add 1 tablespoon of finely-chopped onion and 1 of chopped shallots. Then add $\frac{1}{2}$ lb. of finely chopped mushroom stalks and peelings, previously well squeezed in a cloth so as to extract as much moisture as possible. Mix all thoroughly and cook till all moisture has completely evaporated from the mushrooms. Season with salt and pepper, add a pinch of chopped parsley, put into an earthenware terrine, cover with buttered paper and use as required.

DUXELLES STUFFING (For Tomatoes, Cucumbers, etc.)

To every 4 ozs. of Duxelles in the previous recipe, add 2 ozs. of the soft part of bread, soaked in milk, and dried in a saucepan over a quick fire, and allowed to stand till cold.

DUXELLES STUFFING À LA BONNE FEMME

This can be used for stuffing meat dishes, poultry, vegetables, etc. Add equal parts of sausage meat to the uncooked dry Duxelles (see p. 71) and either cook both together or use uncooked, according to the dish it is intended for. It is always preferable, however, partially to cook this stuffing when it is to be used to stuff a bird, etc.

MUSHROOM STUFFING

Choose small mushrooms, peel them and wash them or clean them with a cloth. Chop them and cook them in a little hot butter, seasoning with salt, a dash of cayenne and a light sprinkling of mace. Mix with half their weight of breadcrumbs, and stir well over a slow fire. Bind with 1 or 2 whole eggs, add 1 teaspoon of grated lemon rind, and a squeeze of lemon juice.

MUSHROOM AND OYSTER STUFFING
(For Poultry)

Prepare 1 lb. or more of mushrooms, as for Duxelles stuffing, with the bread soaked in milk and dried. Put in a pan with a little butter, mix thoroughly, and add a few bearded oysters. Season highly with salt, pepper, and a squeeze of lemon juice. This makes an excellent stuffing for turkey.

A Few Mushroom Ketchups

The mushrooms to be used for Ketchup, if wild, should always be gathered on a dry day. They should not be washed or peeled. Cut off the stalk end which is apt to be earthy, and clean off any earth or dirt with a little salt. Avoid using decayed or worm-eaten mushrooms. When mushrooms first open, the under side is of a pale pinkish colour, which changes to ashy-brown and deepens in colour when the mushroom reaches maturity. In this state mushrooms yield a greater abundance of juice and it is therefore preferable to select fully-grown mushrooms to make Ketchup.

Everything used in the making of Ketchups should be scrupulously clean and *quite dry*. The bottles in which the Ketchup is to be stored should be thoroughly dried, and it is advisable to put them in a cool oven for an hour or so to free them entirely from any moisture. But they should be quite cold before the Ketchup is put into them. The bottles should be fitted with an air-tight stopper or cork.

MUSHROOM KETCHUP (1)

Ingredients: 7 lbs. of freshly-gathered ripe mushrooms, ½ lb. of salt. To each quart of liquor allow $\frac{1}{2}$ oz. of black pepper or $\frac{1}{4}$ teaspoon of cayenne pepper and $\frac{1}{4}$ teaspoon of pounded mace.

Method: Break the mushrooms into small pieces, put them in a deep earthenware pan, and strew with the salt, keeping a larger portion of salt for the top. Let them stand for 2 days, turning them frequently with a wooden spoon. Then put them in a large enamelled saucepan and heat slowly and simmer for 15 to 20 minutes. Now strain the liquor, but without pressing the mushrooms, measure it, and put it into a perfectly clean saucepan and boil until it is reduced by nearly half. Add the seasonings, pour the Ketchup into a clean jug or jar, cover with a cloth and let stand for 24 hours. Then pour it carefully from the sediment into bottles, cork tightly and seal the cork or use bottles with airtight stoppers. Keep in a cool dry place.

MUSHROOM KETCHUP (2)

Ingredients: 7 lbs. of mushrooms, $\frac{1}{2}$ lb. of salt. To each quart of liquor allow $\frac{1}{2}$ oz. of black pepper, $\frac{1}{4}$ oz. of allspice, $\frac{1}{2}$ oz. of ginger, and 2 blades of mace.

Method: Break the mushrooms in small pieces and put them in an earthenware pan and strew with the salt. Cover with a cloth and let stand till the following day. Strain off the liquor, measure it, and boil for 15 minutes. Add the seasonings and simmer for another 20 minutes. When quite cold, put into bottles and seal.

MUSHROOM KETCHUP (3)

Ingredients: 1½ pints of freshly-made Mushroom Ketchup, 1 oz. of shallots, ½ pint of walnut ketchup or pickle, 1 wineglass of cayenne or chili vinegar.

Method: Put the Mushroom Ketchup in a saucepan with small peeled shallots, and simmer for 5 minutes. Then add the other ingredients, bring to the boil, remove at once from the fire and, when cold, bottle it, leaving the shallots in the Ketchup.

MUSHROOM KETCHUP (4)

Proceed as in recipe No. 1 for Mushroom Ketchup, but adding 1 gill of Port wine or Madeira to every quart of Ketchup, when it has been removed from the fire.

MUSHROOM KETCHUP (5)

Proceed as in recipe for Mushroom Ketchup No. 2, but add to the seasoning 2 ozs. of peeled shallots, 2 cloves of garlic, 6 cloves, and 3 or 4 bayleaves. Simmer for 20 minutes as directed.

MUSHROOM KETCHUP (6)

This recipe is taken from Dr. Kitchiner's *The Cook's Oracle* (1823), and I give it in his own

words: "Take care they are the right sort and
fresh gathered. Full grown Flaps are to be
preferred: put a layer of these at the bottom of a
deep earthen pan, and sprinkle them with salt,
then another layer of Mushrooms, and some more
salt on them, and so on alternately, salt and mushrooms; let them remain two or three hours, by
which time the salt will have penetrated the
mushrooms, and rendered them easy to break;
then pound them in a mortar or mash them with
your hands, and let them remain for a couple of
days, not longer, stirring them and mashing them
well each day; then pour them into a stone jar, and
to each quart add one ounce of whole Black Pepper;
stop the jar very close, and set it in a stewpan of
boiling water, and keep it boiling for two hours at
least. Take out the jar, and pour the juice
clear from the settlings through a hair sieve
(without squeezing the mushrooms) into a clean
stewpan; let it boil very gently for half an hour;
those who are for Superlative Catsup will continue
the boiling till the Mushroom juice is reduced to
half the quantity : it may then be called *Double*
CAT-SUP or Dog-sup. Skim it well, and pour it
into a clean dry jar, or jug; cover it close, and let
it stand in a cool place till next day, then pour it
off as gently as possible (so as not to disturb the
settlings at the bottom of the jug) through a
tammis, or thick flannel bag, till it is perfectly
clear; add a tablespoon of good Brandy to each

pint of Catsup, and let it stand as before; a fresh sediment will be deposited, from which the Catsup is to be quietly poured off and bottled in pints or half-pints (which have been washed with Brandy or spirit). Take especial care that it is closely corked and sealed."

Various Ways of Preserving and Pickling Mushrooms

BOTTLED MUSHROOMS (1)

The mushrooms should be freshly gathered and not old. Choose them when they are still quite young and discard any which are not quite sound. Peel the mushrooms carefully, and put them in a large saucepan of boiling salted water (allow ¾ oz. of salt to each quart of water) and boil for 20 minutes. Drain them on a sieve and put them for 1 minute only in cold water which has previously been boiled. Remove from the water and drain them. Now put the mushrooms in glass jars or bottles and completely cover them with cold boiled salted water (¾ oz. to every quart of water) and cork them with sterilised corks—this is done by putting the corks in boiling water to which a little salicylic acid has been added. Now put the jars in a saucepan of boiling water—the water to be just below the level of the corks—and boil for 4 to 5 hours, adding more boiling water so that the water will always be up to the same level.

The bottles must be carefully watched for about 8 days. If no sign of fermentation takes place, the bottling has been successfully accomplished. Mushrooms bottled in this way can be used in the same manner as fresh mushrooms, and should be washed first of all in lukewarm water so that they are not too salty, and then dipped in cold water so that they will become quite firm.

BOTTLED MUSHROOMS (2)

Choose young and perfectly sound mushrooms. Trim and peel them carefully, put in a saucepan, cover with water, add the juice of 1 large lemon to each quart of water, just under 1 oz. of salt, cover the saucepan and bring to the boil. Boil for 3 to 4 minutes. Now put the mushrooms in jars, cover with the liquid in which they were boiled, cork tightly or use jars with air-tight lids, and boil for 1½ hours in a saucepan of boiling water, being careful to replace the water as it boils away.

BOTTLED MUSHROOMS (3)

This method gives quite good results, but the mushrooms cannot be kept for any length of time. Peel the mushrooms, trim the stalks, and wash them thoroughly. Blanch in boiling salted water for 2 or 3 minutes only. Drain and put the mushrooms in a basin of cold water. Drain once more and put the mushrooms in jars, covering them with slightly salted water. Cork the jars tightly, and seal them or use jars with airtight lids. Put the jars in a large saucepan of boiling water, keeping them apart with a little straw, and boil for 30 minutes, adding more boiling water when necessary. Remove the saucepan from the fire, but let the jars stand in it, till the water is quite cold. Wipe and dry the jars carefully, and keep in a cool dry place. The slightly salted water in which they are kept becomes highly flavoured with the mushrooms and can be used to flavour sauces, soups, etc.

PICKLED MUSHROOMS (1)

Wash and dry the mushrooms thoroughly and remove the stalks. Pack them closely in jars or in small tubs, add a few bayleaves, a few shallots or cloves of garlic (optional), and cover with boiling vinegar. Let stand till quite cold, and cork tightly or put on airtight lids.

PICKLED MUSHROOMS (2)

Choose small, freshly gathered mushrooms. They should be quite firm. Peel them and scald them with boiling salted water. Drain thoroughly, and pack them closely in jars, with a few small red chili peppers, 2 or 3 cloves of garlic, or, if preferred, a few very small pickling onions, a few cloves, a good sprinkling of salt, and cover with vinegar, preferably wine vinegar. Cork tightly and stand for about 6 weeks before using.

PICKLED MUSHROOMS (3)

Select freshly-gathered, small and sound button mushrooms. Cut the stems off quite close and, if necessary, clean them with a slightly moistened cloth, dipped in salt. Put them in a basin of cold salted water, drain quickly, and dry thoroughly. To every quart of mushrooms allow just under 1 quart of *White Wine vinegar*—the flavour of the pickle is much better and the mushrooms will remain much whiter. Add to this 1 heaped teaspoon of salt, $\frac{1}{2}$ oz. of whole white pepper, 1 oz. of ginger, sliced or slightly bruised, $\frac{1}{2}$ saltspoon of cayenne, which should all be tied in a small piece of muslin, with 2 blades of mace. Bring the vinegar, with the seasonings, to the boil, put in the mushrooms, and boil for 6 to 8 minutes, according to their size. Put them into warmed jars, cover with the vinegar and spices, and let stand till quite cold. Then cork tightly or screw on airtight lids, and store in a cool, dry place.

MUSHROOMS PRESERVED IN OIL OR FAT (1)

In the south of France, mushrooms are preserved in either olive oil, melted fat or butter. They are washed and cooked for 3 or 4 minutes only in the same manner as for a Garnish (see p. 38), thoroughly drained and dried, and then put into clean glass or stone jars, and covered with either oil, melted fat or butter. This should have a depth of about 1½ to 2 inches above the mushrooms. The jars should then be well corked and sealed and kept in a cool, dry place.

MUSHROOMS IN OIL (2)

Choose small young mushrooms, peel them and remove the stalks, which should also be peeled. Wash the mushrooms in a little white wine or water. Drain them and put in a saucepan, and cover them liberally with olive oil, flavoured with 2 or 3 bayleaves, 4 or 5 cloves, salt and peppercorns. Simmer for 20 minutes, then add 2 tablespoons of vinegar and simmer for another 10 minutes. Remove the saucepan from the fire and let stand till quite cold. Now pack the mushrooms into jars, strain the liquid over them, and cork tightly. These can be served as a cold hors-d'œuvre, or can be used in sauces, etc.

MUSHROOMS IN OIL (3)

Choose small mushrooms, trim the stalks, wash them with a damp sponge and cook for 3 or 4 minutes as directed in Mushrooms as a Garnish (see p. 38). Drain and dry them thoroughly, put them in jars, cork tightly, and put the jars in a saucepan of water, wrapping each jar in a cloth, so that they will not touch each other. Bring to the boil and boil for 30 minutes. Remove from the water only when cold, dry the jars, and use the mushrooms as required.

MUSHROOMS AND TOMATOES IN JARS

Choose small mushrooms, trim the stalks, wash and thoroughly drain the mushrooms, and cook them as for a Garnish, but for 3 or 4 minutes only. Drain again, pack them in jars and cover with the following : Choose large and ripe tomatoes, quarter them and put in a saucepan with a bayleaf or two, bring gradually to the boil, crushing the tomatoes with a wooden spoon. Season with salt, a little pepper, and a pinch of sugar (optional). Simmer till the tomatoes are reduced to a pulp—which will take about 1 hour or longer, according to the ripeness of the tomatoes. Then rub through a sieve and pour over the mushrooms. Cork the jars tightly and seal them, or use jars having airtight lids, and put in a saucepan with water reaching almost to the level of the corks. Bring to the boil and boil for about 1 hour. Remove the saucepan from the fire, and let the jars stand in the water till quite cold. Dry, and store in a cool, dry place.

MUSHROOMS IN MADEIRA

Choose medium-sized mushrooms, trim the stalks and wash the mushrooms. Put the mushrooms in a saucepan, cover them with Madeira, add a pinch of salt, put the lid on the saucepan, and gradually bring to the boil. Simmer very gently for 10 minutes. Remove the saucepan from the fire, and let stand till quite cold. Then pack the mushrooms in jars, pour the Madeira over them, cork tightly or use airtight lids, and proceed as in the foregoing recipe.

DRIED MUSHROOMS

Small mushrooms can be dried whole, but large ones should be peeled, the stalks removed, and cut in thick slices, or quartered. There are various methods of drying mushrooms. They can be placed on frames of wire-netting or basket-work of some kind, not too close to each other, as they must not be in contact. These frames should be kept in the shade in a very dry place.

They can also be strung on string, but again, care must be taken that they are not close to each other. They are then hung in a shady and somewhat draughty place.

Mushrooms can also be dried in a cool oven.

Mushrooms may take only a few days to dry, or a few weeks, according to the humidity in the air, and to various other factors. When quite dried, they can be stored in sacks or paper bags, which should be shaken occasionally, or they can be kept in jars with close-fitting lids, and stored in a cool, dry place.

Before using dried mushrooms they should be soaked in lukewarm water for about 1 hour, and can then be cooked and used in the same way as fresh mushrooms.

MUSHROOM POWDER (1)

When once the mushrooms are dried by any of the methods described in the foregoing recipe, they can be pounded in a mortar and then rubbed through a sieve. Put the mushroom powder in jars having airtight lids, and store in a cool, dry place. This mushroom powder makes an excellent flavouring for sauces, stews, soups, etc.

MUSHROOM POWDER (2)

Choose medium-sized or somewhat large mushrooms, wipe them clean with a cloth dipped in salt, and remove the stalks. Put them in a saucepan with 2 large onions, stuck with 3 or 4 cloves, 3 or 4 tablespoons of salt (preferably coarse salt), a quarter of a teaspoon of mace, and 2 teaspoons of black pepper. Do not add any liquid of any sort. Simmer very gently till the liquor which the mushrooms and onion produce has completely evaporated, being very careful, however, that the mushrooms do not burn. Then put them on wire-netting frames in a shady and very dry place to dry, or dry them in a cool oven. When quite dry, pound in a mortar, rub through a sieve, and put them in jars, as in the previous recipe.

MUSHROOMS PRESERVED IN SALT

Trim the mushrooms, clean with a dry cloth dipped in salt, and pack in jars, with a thick layer of salt (preferably coarse salt) between each layer of mushrooms. Cover the whole with more salt, and cork tightly. Mushrooms preserved in this way will not keep for more than a few months.

SALTED MUSHROOMS À LA RUSSE

Prepare the mushrooms as in the last recipe. Pack them in jars, sprinkling each layer with salt, uncooked chopped onion and a few peppercorns. Cork tightly and store in a cool, dry place.

Mushroom Soups

MUSHROOM PURÉE

Wash the mushrooms, dry them and cook as for a Garnish (see p. 38), but cook them till quite soft. Rub through a sieve, but keep the water in which they were boiled. Put the mushrooms in a saucepan and dilute with the liquid in which they were cooked and a little hot milk. Generally speaking, the quantity of liquid should be about double that of the sieved mushrooms. Stir well, season with salt and pepper, and simmer for a few minutes. Remove the saucepan from the fire, and stir in 2½ to 3 ozs. of butter, divided in small pieces. Serve with croûtons of fried bread.

MUSHROOM VELOUTÉ

Cook the mushrooms as for a Garnish (see p. 38), drain thoroughly and rub through a sieve. Keep the water in which the mushrooms were cooked. In a small thick saucepan work 1 oz. of butter with just under 1 oz. of flour and, when quite smooth, dilute with 1½ pints of the water in which the mushrooms were cooked and ½ pint of light stock, stirring continuously. Bring to the boil, skim carefully, add the sieved mushrooms, 2 or 3 sprigs of chopped parsley, season with salt and pepper and simmer for $\frac{3}{4}$ of an hour. A few minutes before serving, mix the yolks of 2 eggs in a basin with 4 or 5 tablespoons of cream, add a few tablespoons of the hot soup, then add the whole to the soup, stirring well, but do not allow to boil. Remove the saucepan from the fire, and add $2\frac{1}{2}$ to 3 ozs. of butter, divided in small pieces. Stir till the butter has melted and serve with either croûtons of fried bread, or with diced cooked mushrooms.

The proportions are 2 parts of the velouté to 1 of the sieved mushrooms, and 1 of light stock, including the cream. To every quart of soup, allow the yolks of 2 or 3 eggs, 4 to 6 tablespoons of cream and finally $2\frac{1}{2}$ to 3 ozs. of butter.

MUSHROOM CREAM

The preparation of this is the same as that of the Mushroom Velouté, but a thin Béchamel Sauce (see p. 69) is used to dilute the mushroom purée. The proportions are identical, but the yolks of egg are omitted, and 6 tablespoons of cream are added finally.

CRÈME AGNES SOREL

Wash and peel 1 lb. of mushrooms and rub them through a sieve. Put in a saucepan, stir in gradually 1 pint of thin Béchamel Sauce (see p. 69), and simmer for about 8 minutes. Then add $1\frac{1}{2}$ pints of Cream of Chicken, and stir over a slow fire till very hot, but do not allow to boil. Just before serving, add 4 tablespoons of cream. The garnish consists of thin strips of cooked mushrooms, thin strips of cooked breast of chicken and thin strips of tongue.

Cream of Chicken is made in the same manner as Mushroom Cream, but the foundation purée, instead of being made with mushrooms, consists of cooked chicken, first pounded in a mortar and then rubbed through a sieve.

DRIED MUSHROOM SOUP À LA RUSSE

Soak ¾ lb. of dried mushrooms for 1 hour in cold water. Drain thoroughly, chop them coarsely, and put in a saucepan with sufficient water to cover them amply. Add 1 sliced onion, 1 sliced carrot, 1 leek, mixed herbs, and season with salt and a few peppercorns. Bring to the boil and simmer very gently for 2 hours. Strain the soup through a sieve and serve with a garnish of thinly sliced cooked mushrooms. This mushroom stock is excellent to use as a flavouring with either ordinary meat stock, or with some vegetable or fish soups.

DRIED MUSHROOM SOUP À LA JUIVE

Put 2 lbs. of thickly sliced potatoes in a saucepan with 1 large onion, ½ lb. of sliced large, dried mushrooms, season with salt and pepper, cover with water and bring to the boil. Simmer for 1 hour, stirring occasionally. This is a popular soup among Russian Jews.

HUNGARIAN MUSHROOM SOUP

Wash and dry thoroughly ½ lb. of mushrooms. Slice them and put in a saucepan with 1 table-spoon of butter, and sprinkle with 1 tablespoon of paprika. Simmer very slowly for 10 to 15 minutes, but without browning. Then add 1 tablespoon of flour and stir till the flour is lightly coloured. Add gradually, stirring continuously, 2 pints of boiling stock, bring to the boil and simmer for 1 hour. A few minutes before serving, beat the yolk of 1 egg with 6 tablespoons of sour cream, add 2 or 3 tablespoons of the hot stock, and, when well mixed, add this to the soup and stir, but do not allow to boil.

MUSHROOM JULIENNE

This consists of mushrooms, cut into thin strips not more than 1½ inches in length, added to boiling stock or consommé 20 minutes before serving. Just before serving, add also to the soup a few croûtons of fried bread.

POLISH MUSHROOM SOUP

Pour boiling water over 4 ozs. of dried mush-rooms and let them stand for a few minutes. Drain and put them in 2 quarts of boiling meat or vegetable stock, and cook till tender. When done, remove them from the stock, chop them coarsely and return to the stock. Melt 2 ozs. of butter in a small saucepan, stir in 2 ozs. of potato flour, cook for a few minutes, but without browning, dilute with a few tablespoons of hot stock, and stir this mixture into the soup. Season with salt and pepper, and a few minutes before serving add 6 tablespoons of sour cream.

MUSHROOM SOUP À LA VIENNOISE

Slice 1 lb. of mushrooms, and put in a saucepan with 2 ozs. of butter, 1 chopped medium-sized onion, and simmer very gently for 10 minutes, but without browning. Then add 1 or 2 quartered tomatoes and cook till quite soft. Add 1 gill of boiling water and simmer for 20 minutes. Rub all through a sieve, put the purée in a saucepan, with the liquid in which the mushrooms, onion and tomatoes were cooked, and dilute to the right consistency with boiling cream, seasoning with salt and pepper. Stir well, and simmer for another 5 minutes.

Fish

FISH MATELOTE À LA NORMANDE

The distinguishing feature of this dish is the use of cider, as in most dishes which hail from Normandy, instead of the usual red or white wine.

Ingredients: 2 lbs. altogether of the following fish: small eels, sole and gurnet; 1¼ pints of cider, 4 ozs. of onion, 1 clove of garlic, ½ pint of fish stock, 1 oz. of flour, 1 oz. of butter, 1 gill of cream to every pint of sauce, 1 liqueur glass of brandy (in Normandy, Calvados or brandy made from apples, is used), mixed herbs, salt and pepper. For the garnish: ½ lb. of mushrooms, mussels, oysters, a few Dublin prawns, croûtons of fried bread.

Method: Put the sliced onion in a large saucepan with the fish, cut in 3 inch lengths, the chopped herbs, garlic and a little salt. Cover with the cider, add the brandy, bring to the boil, and cook for about 15 minutes. Remove the pieces of fish from the liquid, and strain the latter through a sieve into another saucepan. Let it boil till reduced by one third. Then add the flour and butter, first worked to a smooth paste in a small saucepan and gradually diluted with the hot ½ pint of fish stock—the whole having been simmered till it thickens. Then add the warmed cream and stir well. Pile the pieces of fish in the centre of a hot dish, pour the sauce over them and garnish with the mushrooms, previously cooked (see Mushrooms as a Garnish, p. 38), the cooked mussels, the bearded oysters and the shelled Dublin prawns and croûtons.

FILLETS OF SOLE BOITELLE

Ingredients: To every 4 small fillets of sole allow 6 tablespoons of strong fish stock, 2 ozs. of butter, 4 ozs. of mushrooms, salt, pepper, and 1 tablespoon of lemon juice.

Method: Trim the fillets of sole neatly, roll them and put them in a well buttered fireproof dish, with the chopped mushrooms, the fish stock, the lemon juice, and season well with salt and pepper. Cover the dish, and put in a very moderate oven and simmer, without ever boiling, for about 15 minutes, or till the fish is quite tender. Put the fish on a hot dish, with the mushrooms in the centre of the dish, stir 1 oz. of butter, divided into small pieces, into the liquid in which the fish was cooked, and pour this over the whole.

FISH CROQUETTES

Ingredients: To every ½ lb. of cooked, boned and chopped white fish allow ¼ lb. of chopped cooked mushrooms, a few tablespoons of thick Béchamel Sauce to bind (see p. 69), flour, yolk of egg, fine white breadcrumbs.

Method: Put the chopped, cooked fish in a basin and mix thoroughly with the chopped mushrooms, cooked as for a Garnish (see p. oo). Bind with a few tablespoons of thick Béchamel Sauce, well seasoned, to which 1 or 2 tablespoons of the liquid in which the mushrooms have cooked should be added. Let stand till quite cold. Then shape into small cork-shaped croquettes, roll in flour, coat with beaten yolk of egg, and with fine white breadcrumbs, and fry to a light golden colour in very hot oil. Drain, put on a hot dish, on a folded napkin, and serve with either a White Mushroom Sauce (see p. 66) or another appropriate sauce.

FISH "TOURTE À LA RUSSE"

Ingredients: 1 lb. of pie crust, $\frac{1}{2}$ lb. of sliced salmon, 4 fillets of sole or whiting, $\frac{1}{2}$ lb. of chopped cooked white fish, 3 or 4 anchovies, $\frac{3}{4}$ lb. of mushrooms, a few shelled prawns, Béchamel Sauce.

Method: Roll the pastry out to a large round, about $\frac{1}{2}$ inch thick. Mix the cooked and chopped white fish with the chopped anchovies and a little Béchamel Sauce to bind. Put this in the centre of the pastry, leaving a clear edge of pastry, so that it can be raised to cover the "tourte" when it is fully garnished. Over this fish forcemeat, lay the sliced salmon and fillets of sole or whiting, previously lightly cooked in butter with a little lemon juice. Cover with the chopped mushrooms, cooked as for a Garnish (see p. 38), then mixed with a little Béchamel Sauce and a few shelled prawns. Gather the pastry over the ingredients, till it meets on the top, and press firmly together, damping the édges, and leaving a small opening in the middle. Brush over with beaten yolk of egg and bake in a moderate oven to a light golden colour.

HERRINGS À LA CALAISIENNE

This is a most delicious way of preparing fresh herrings. Split the back of the herrings and carefully remove the backbone and bones. Put the roes in a basin and work with a little butter, chopped parsley, 1 oz. of chopped shallot and 1 oz. of finely-chopped mushrooms to every 2 small herrings. Cook the herrings lightly in butter for a few minutes only, then stuff with the mixture, wrap them in oiled foolscap paper and cook in a moderate oven for about 10 to 12 minutes, according to the size of the fish. Unwrap and put on a hot dish.

SALMON WITH MUSHROOMS

Ingredients: Slices of salmon about $\frac{1}{2}$ inch thick, 2 large mushrooms and 12 prawns to each slice of salmon, Poulette Sauce (see p. 66).

Method: Put the salmon in a fireproof, somewhat shallow dish, and barely cover with equal parts of white wine and water, season with salt and peppercorns. Bring to the boil and simmer gently for 15 to 20 minutes, or a little longer, till the fish is tender. When done, drain, put on a hot dish and garnish with the mushrooms, previously cooked as for a Garnish (see p. 38). Over each mushroom put a few shelled prawns, and cover the whole with Poulette Sauce.

SOLE À LA BONNE FEMME

Ingredients: A 2 lb. sole, or 2 soles, each weighing 1 lb., ¾ lb. of mushrooms, 1 oz. of chopped shallot, 5 ozs. of butter, 1 teaspoon of flour, 1½ gills of white wine, 6 tablespoons of fish stock, 1 teaspoon of parsley, salt and pepper.

Method: Use a large oblong and somewhat shallow fireproof dish. Butter it generously, sprinkle with the chopped shallot, parsley and mushrooms, and over this lay the fish, with the white side uppermost. Season with salt and pepper, and add the wine and the fish stock—if no fish stock is available, use water. Dot with 1 oz. of butter, divided into small pieces. Bring to the boil, then put in a moderate oven and simmer gently for about 20 minutes, basting every 5 to 6 minutes. Remove the dish from the fire, tilt it, and carefully pour the liquid into a small thick saucepan. Rapidly reduce it to one gill, thickening it with the flour worked with ½ oz. of butter. Remove the saucepan from the fire, add the remaining butter, divided into small pieces, and whisk rapidly. Meanwhile, the fish, mushrooms, etc., should have been kept warm in the oven. Pour the sauce over the fish just before serving.

TROUT EN PAPILLOTE

The trout should be quite small ones—about 3 to the pound—and thoroughly cleaned and split open on the belly side. Season with salt and pepper, sprinkle with a little flour, and cook in hot clarified butter for 5 to 6 minutes, turning the fish once. Remove from the frying pan, and inside each fish put a little Duxelles Stuffing (see p. 64), moistened with a little Béchamel Sauce. Wrap the fish in oiled plain foolscap paper, and place in a slow oven till the paper begins to brown. Serve wrapped in the paper. The paper for this should be prepared from the whole double sheet of full-sized foolscap. Cut into the shape of a large heart, the folded foolscap being the middle of the heart. Place the fish with the tail end pointing to the bottom of the paper, in a slightly slanting position. Fold the paper over it, then crinkle the edges with the fingers, so that the paper will not come undone.

TURBOT À LA BOURGUIGNONNE

For a turbot weighing about 2½ lbs. allow ¾ lb. of mushrooms, and sufficient red wine to half cover the fish, a bouquet of mixed herbs, and about 4 ozs. of butter, salt and pepper.

Method: Put the fish in a well-buttered dish,

sprinkle with the chopped mushrooms, add the mixed herbs, the red wine and a small piece of butter. Cover the dish and braise the fish in a very slow oven, basting often. The time will depend on the thickness of the fish—about 30 minutes will be sufficient, if the fish is constantly basted. Now put the fish on a hot dish and keep warm in the oven. Strain the sauce into a small saucepan, reduce it a little over a quick fire, and thicken with 1 teaspoon of flour worked with a little butter. Remove the saucepan from the fire and whisk in rapidly the remaining butter, divided into small pieces. Pour the sauce over the fish and serve.

WHITING AU GRATIN

Put a layer of Duxelles Sauce (see p. 64) in a shallow fireproof dish, and over this place the number of fillets of whiting required. Cover with another layer of sauce, sprinkle with breadcrumbs, pour 1 or 2 tablespoons of melted butter over the whole, and put in a moderate oven for about 20 minutes, till the fish is quite tender and the breadcrumbs are lightly browned..

Meat

BEEF À LA BOURGUIGNONNE

Ingredients: 4 lbs. of top rump of beef, 6 ozs. of larding bacon. For the marinade: 1¼ pints of red wine, 1 medium-sized onion, 1 bayleaf, a few springs of parsley and thyme, 2 tablespoons of oil, salt and pepper. For the cooking of the beef: 3 tablespoons of butter or fat, 1 oz. of flour, ¾ pint of light stock, 1 oz. of mushroom peelings and stalks, mixed herbs, 1 clove of garlic. For the garnish: 1 lb. of mushrooms, ½ lb. of lean gammon, 24 pickling onions, 3½ ozs. of butter.

Method: Cut the larding bacon into thin strips and lard the beef. Slice the onion, and put half of it, with some of the herbs, in an earthenware terrine or casserole, just sufficiently large to hold the meat. Put the meat over the onion, sprinkle freely with salt, a little pepper, cover with the rest of the onion and herbs, and add the oil and the red wine. Let stand in a cool place for several hours, or even overnight. Do not touch or turn the meat.

Now remove the beef from the marinade, and dry thoroughly with a cloth. Melt the butter or fat in a thick saucepan and, when very hot, put in the meat, and brown it equally on all sides. Take the meat out, and stir in the flour, letting it brown. Then dilute gradually with the hot stock, and the strained wine of the marinade. Replace the meat in the saucepan, with the herb bouquet, the garlic, and the chopped mushroom peelings and stalks. Cover, bring to the boil and boil for 5 minutes. Then put the saucepan in a slow oven and simmer for 3½ hours—on no account should the liquid be on the full boil.

While the meat is cooking, the garnish can be prepared. Peel the mushrooms, remove the stalks, and cook them in a little butter, seasoning with salt and pepper. Drain, and set aside till required.

Peel the onions carefully, and lightly brown them in a little butter, drain, and also set aside. Cut the gammon into ½ inch cubes, put them in a saucepan, cover with cold water, bring to the boil and cook for 5 minutes. Drain, and brown them lightly in butter.

Remove the meat from the saucepan, strain the sauce into a basin, rinse the saucepan with hot water, and replace the meat in it. Add the strained sauce, the mushrooms, onions and cubes of gammon, bring to the boil and simmer for 15 minutes. To serve, put the meat on a hot dish, surround with the garnish, pour some of the sauce over it and serve the rest of the sauce in a sauce-boat.

BEEF AU GRATIN

This dish is done with somewhat thick slices of cooked beef. Put a coating of Duxelles Sauce (see p. 64) in a shallow fireproof dish, lay the slices of cooked beef over it, cover with Duxelles Sauce, sprinkle with breadcrumbs, and moisten with 2 tablespoons of melted butter. Put in a brisk oven to brown lightly. Serve in the same dish.

FILLET OF BEEF WITH MUSHROOMS

Ingredients: 3 lbs. of fillet of beef, 1 lb. of large mushrooms, ¼ of a lb. of small buttom mushrooms, 1 wineglass of Madeira, butter, salt and pepper.

Method: Rub the meat with salt and sprinkle with a little pepper. Put it in a roasting pan, on a grid, and cover the whole surface of the meat with butter. Put in a brisk oven for 6 to 8 minutes, then cook in a moderate oven, allowing about 10 minutes to the lb. The fillet should always be somewhat underdone. Baste every 6 to 8 minutes with butter. Peel and remove the stalks of the large mushrooms, and cook as for a Garnish (see p. 38). When the beef is ready, put it on a hot dish, mix the Madeira with the bastings in the pan, pour over the meat, and garnish with the mushrooms. Serve with a Mushroom Sauce (see p. 66) to which the button mushrooms, also previously cooked as for a Garnish, have been added.

FILLET OF BEEF RICHELIEU

Cook the fillet of beef in the same manner as in the foregoing recipe. When done, put on a hot dish and surround with mushrooms, stuffed à la Bordelaise (see p. 59), small tomatoes, filled with thick Duxelles Sauce (see p. 64), and at each end of the dish put some braised lettuce. Strain the butter which has been used for basting through a coarse sieve and serve it in a sauceboat.

TOURNEDOS

Tournedos are small steaks cut from the fillet, and neatly trimmed of all fat and gristle. They should be about 1 inch thick, 2 inches in diameter and should weigh about 3 to $3\frac{1}{2}$ ozs. each. Melt a little butter in a deep frying pan and, when hot, put in the tournedos and season with salt and a little pepper. Cook till lightly browned on one side, then turn them, and cook the other side. They should be kept underdone. Put them on a hot dish when done and cover with Chasseur Sauce (see p. 63).

TOURNEDOS WITH MUSHROOMS

Cook the tournedos in the same manner as in the previous recipe. When done, arrange neatly around a hot dish, and in the centre of the dish put 1 lb. of small mushrooms, previously cooked in butter, well seasoned with salt and pepper, and a sprinkling of lemon juice. Over each tournedos put a large mushroom, cooked in the same manner. Moisten with a little Espagnole Sauce (see p. 65).

BRAISED CALVES' LIVER WITH MUSHROOMS

Ingredients: 1½ lbs. of calves' liver, ¼ lb. of larding bacon, 3 or 4 rashers of fat bacon. For the marinade: 1 large onion, ½ pint of white wine, 2 tablespoons of oil, a few sprigs of parsley, thyme, 1 bayleaf, salt and peppercorns. For cooking the liver: ¾ pint of stock, the marinade, 3 small tomatoes, 1 oz. of butter, just under 1 oz. of flour. For the garnish: 1 lb. of mushrooms.

Method: Cut the larding bacon into thin strips and lard the liver with these. Put half of the ingredients for the marinade—the onion should be finely chopped—in a deep dish, place the liver over them, season with salt and pepper, and cover with the rest of the onion, herbs, the oil and wine. Let stand in a cool place for about 2 hours, turning the liver occasionally. Then remove it from the marinade, dry thoroughly in a cloth, and wrap it in the bacon rashers. Put the butter in a saucepan—the saucepan should be a thick one and just sufficiently large to hold the liver—and, when hot, put in the liver, and cook till lightly browned on both sides. Now put the liver on a plate, and mix the flour with the butter, stirring till it browns. Add the hot stock, the marinade, the chopped tomatoes, bring to the boil, stirring continuously. Put in the liver, cover the saucepan and simmer in a very slow oven for 2 hours. Half an hour before serving, strain the sauce, put back in the saucepan with the liver, and add the mushrooms, peeled and previously lightly tossed in butter for a few minutes only.

FRICASSÉE OF VEAL

Ingredients: 2½ lbs. of lean veal, 1½ pints of water, 2 ozs. of chopped onions, 1 large onion, stuck with a clove, mixed herbs, a small stick of celery, just under 1 tablespoon of salt. For the sauce: 1½ ozs. of butter, 1 oz. of flour, ¾ pint of the veal stock, 1 tablespoon of mushroom peelings, the yolks of 2 eggs, 6 tablespoons of cream, the juice of 1 lemon, 1 teaspoon of chopped parsley. For the garnish: ¾ lb. of small button mushrooms, 12 pickling onions, 1 oz. of butter.

Method: Remove all fat and gristle from the meat, and cut the veal in 2 inch lengths. Put it in a saucepan and add the cold water and salt. Bring to the boil and skim carefully. When the scum has ceased to rise, and the surface of the liquid is entirely free from grease, add the onion, the carrots, the celery and herbs. Bring to the boil, cover the saucepan, leaving a small opening, and simmer for 1 to 1½ hours. The meat should be tender but quite firm. When done, remove the pieces of veal from the saucepan, and strain the sauce into a basin. In a small saucepan, melt the butter and stir in the flour gradually, but without browning, and dilute with ¾ pint of the hot veal stock, stirring continuously. Bring to the boil, add the mushroom peelings, and a few peppercorns. Skim carefully, and add the eggs, previously mixed in a basin with the lemon juice and a few tablespoons of stock. Then add the cream. Put the veal in a saucepan, pour the sauce over it, add the mushrooms, peeled and lightly cooked in butter, the onions, also cooked in butter but without browning, and simmer very gently for about 20 minutes, but without ever allowing the sauce to be on the full boil. The sauce should not be too thick—it should be of the consistency of thin cream. To serve, put the pieces of veal in the centre of the dish, pour the sauce over them, and garnish with the mushrooms and onions. Sprinkle with chopped parsley.

PAUPIETTES OF VEAL WITH MUSHROOMS

The French word "paupiette" is the equivalent of the English word "collop," a thin slice of lean meat. The veal collops for this dish are cut from the fillet and should be about 5 inches in length and 2½ inches wide. Coat each collop with a thin layer of Mushroom Stuffing (see p. 72), then carefully roll it, surround with a piece of larding bacon, and tie with string. Put 1 oz. of butter in a saucepan, with 3 or 4 rashers of bacon, 1 or 2 sliced carrots, onions, a small stick of celery and lightly brown the vegetables. Next add the paupiettes and also brown lightly, turning them so that they are equally coloured on all sides. Then half cover them with stock, bring to the boil, cover the saucepan and simmer in a very slow oven for 1½ hours. When done, remove the string and larding bacon, put the paupiettes on a hot dish, in the centre of the dish pile up mushrooms, previously cooked as for a Garnish (see p. 38), strain a little of the stock in which the paupiettes were cooked over the whole, and serve with a brown Mushroom Sauce (see p. 66).

VEAL CUTLETS EN PAPILLOTES

Either grill the veal cutlets or brown them in butter, seasoning with salt and pepper. According to the number of cutlets, cut full-sized sheets of plain foolscap paper into large heart shapes, allowing one to each cutlet. Brush one side of the paper with oil or melted butter, lay a thin slice of ham on one half, cover with a layer of thick Duxelles Sauce (see p. 64), over this place the cutlet with the bone end towards the lower end of the heart-shaped sheet of paper. Coat the cutlet with Duxelles Sauce, and cover with another slice of ham. Fold the paper over, crinkle the edges, so that they cannot come undone, and put in a moderate oven till the paper begins to brown. Serve in the paper papillotes.

ESCALOPES OF VEAL WITH MUSHROOMS

Cut thin slices from a fillet of veal, and trim neatly into oval shapes, removing all fat and skin. Each escalope should weigh about 3 to $3\frac{1}{2}$ ozs.

Coat them with a very thick Duxelles Sauce, sprinkle them with flour, coat with yolk of egg and fine white breadcrumbs, and again sprinkle with flour, and coat with egg and breadcrumbs. Fry them in butter to a light golden colour, and serve with a Mushroom Sauce (see p. 66), either brown or white, according to taste.

VEAL SAUTÉ MARENGO

Ingredients: 2 lbs. of lean veal, 1 lb. of chopped tomatoes, 1 large onion, 6 tablespoons of white wine, 1 pint of stock, 3 tablespoons of oil, $\frac{1}{2}$ oz. of flour, 12 pickling onions, $\frac{3}{4}$ lb. of small mushrooms, 1 clove of garlic, salt and pepper.

Method: Put the oil in a saucepan and, when very hot, add the sliced onion and the veal, cut in 2 inch lengths, all fat and gristle having been removed. Brown both onion and veal. Then pour out the oil, add the white wine and let this reduce almost completely. Cover with the hot stock, and add the chopped tomatoes and the garlic and mixed herbs. Bring to the boil and simmer very gently for $1\frac{1}{2}$ hours. Now put the pieces of veal in another saucepan, reduce the sauce by about one-third and strain it over the veal. Add the onions, lightly browned in butter, and the mushrooms, cooked as for a Garnish (see p. 38), and simmer for another 15 minutes. Garnish with croûtons of fried bread.

LAMB CUTLETS MURILLO

Season the number of cutlets required with salt and pepper, and slightly brown one side only in a little hot butter. Remove from the pan, and coat the uncooked side with finely chopped cooked mushrooms moistened with a little Béchamel Sauce (see p. 69). Put them in a fireproof dish, pour a little melted butter over them, and brown in a brisk oven. Put the cutlets on a hot dish and surround with a thick Tomato Sauce.

LAMB CUTLETS À LA PROVENÇALE

Proceed as in the foregoing recipe, but coat the cutlets with finely chopped mushrooms mixed with chopped tomatoes and moistened with a little thick Duxelles Sauce (see p. 64). Finish cooking in the oven. When done, put the cutlets on a hot dish, and over each put a small grilled mushroom, the gills uppermost, and on each mushroom put a stoned olive. Serve with a Tomato Sauce flavoured with a little garlic.

LAMB KIDNEYS SAUTÉS WITH MUSHROOMS

Ingredients: Allow 2 lamb kidneys to each person, and 6 small mushrooms. 1 glass of white wine, 1 level tablespoon of flour, butter, 1 bayleaf, lemon juice, salt and pepper.

Method: Remove the fat and skin from the kidneys and cut in very thin slices. Melt the butter in a sauté pan and, when very hot, put in the sliced kidneys, the bayleaf and season with salt and pepper. Cook for a few minutes on a brisk fire, shaking the pan, and turning the kidneys with a spoon. When nearly done—they should not take longer than 8 to 10 minutes to do—sprinkle with a little flour, stir it in well, then remove the pan from the fire, and add the white wine. Replace the pan on the fire, stir for 2 or 3 minutes and add the mushrooms (see Mushrooms with Butter and Lemon, p. 30) and mix. Serve very hot.

STUFFED SHOULDER OF LAMB OR MUTTON

Stuff a boned shoulder of lamb or mutton with a Mushroom Stuffing (see p. 72) and sew up carefully. Roast it, basting frequently with butter, and, when done, serve with a Duxelles Sauce (see p. 64).

HAM À LA BOURGUIGNONNE

Ingredients: 1 ham, 3 or 4 carrots, 3 or 4 onions, 2 heaped tablespoons of mushroom peelings, 4 large mushrooms, 1 bottle of white wine, a few sprigs of parsley.

Method: Put the ham in a ham kettle and cover with cold water. Bring to the boil and simmer till three-quarters cooked, allowing 20 minutes to the pound. Remove from the water, drain thoroughly, take off the rind and trim off some of the fat. Put the ham in a saucepan in which it just fits, over the chopped carrots, onions and mushroom peeling and parsley, all previously cooked in butter till tender. Cover with the white wine, put the lid on the saucepan and simmer in a very slow oven till done. Strain the sauce through a piece of butter muslin, pressing down the vegetables with the back of a spoon to extract the juice. Add the sliced and previously cooked mushrooms to the sauce.

PORK CHOPS À LA MILANAISE

Trim the chops neatly and flatten with a beater. Season with salt and pepper, sprinkle with flour, then coat with beaten yolk of egg and fine white breadcrumbs. Fry in hot clarified butter till a golden colour. They should be cooked somewhat slowly. When done, put on a hot dish, and in the centre of the dish put ½ lb. of macaroni, previously boiled and drained, mixed with ½ lb. of cooked sliced mushrooms, ¼ lb. of ham, cut in thin strips, the same of smoked tongue, and 1 oz. of grated Parmesan cheese, the whole moistened with a little Tomato Sauce. Serve with a thin Tomato Sauce in a sauceboat.

PORK SAUSAGES WITH MUSHROOMS

Prick about 12 small pork sausages with a fork, and cook them in a few tablespoons of hot lard, but not on too hot a fire. Turn them occasionally so that they will be browned on all sides. When done, remove them from the pan and put them on a plate. Chop 1 large onion and brown this in the same lard, then sprinkle with flour, and stir till brown. Add just under 1 pint of hot stock, 1 or 2 tablespoons of thick Tomato Sauce, 1 clove of garlic, finely chopped, and 1 bayleaf. Cook somewhat briskly for a few minutes to reduce the sauce. Then add the sausages and 1 lb. of sliced mushrooms, previously cooked in butter. Season highly with salt and pepper, mix well and cook for another 5 minutes.

STUFFED SUCKING PIG

The sucking pig should not be more than 5 to 6 weeks old. Stuff it with a Mushroom Stuffing (see p. 72) and sew up neatly. Rub it well over with salt, coat with a little melted butter and cook in a brisk oven for the first 10 minutes, and then in a moderate oven. Baste every 10 minutes, and allow from 20 to 25 minutes to the pound. Serve with a brown Mushroom Sauce (see p. 66).

Poultry

CHICKEN EN COCOTE WITH MUSHROOMS

Melt 3 ozs. of butter in an earthenware casserole and, when very hot, put in the chicken, season with salt and pepper, and brown the chicken, turning it frequently so that it browns on all sides. Then cover the casserole, put in a moderate oven, and cook slowly for about 1 hour or more, according to the size of the chicken, basting frequently. Ten minutes before serving, add 1 lb. of small mushrooms, cooked as for a Garnish (see p. 38), and a few tablespoons of veal or chicken stock. To serve, remove the chicken from the casserole, carve it and put the pieces back in the casserole.

CHICKEN FRICASSÉE

Carve the chicken into joints, and proceed as in recipe for Fricassée of Veal (page 104).

CHICKEN SAUTÉ BERCY

Choose a young tender chicken and divide into 8 joints. Put 2 or 3 ozs. of butter in a deep frying pan and, when very hot put in the pieces of chicken. Cook on a quick fire for 4 or 5 minutes, seasoning the chicken with salt and pepper. Then cook on a slower fire, turning the pieces of chicken occasionally, and cooking to a light golden colour. When done, remove from the pan and keep hot while the sauce is being made.

Pour off a little of the butter from the pan, if there seems an excess of it, and lightly brown 1 tablespoon of finely chopped shallot in it. Then add 6 tablespoons of white wine, 3 tablespoons of meat glaze, the juice of $\frac{1}{2}$ a lemon and 2 ozs. of butter. Stir well and add a few blanched and sliced chipolata sausages and 6 ozs. of chopped cooked mushrooms. Cover the pieces of chicken with this sauce and sprinkle with chopped parsley.

CHICKEN SAUTÉ MARENGO

Cut the chicken into neat joints, and proceed as in making Veal Sauté Marengo (see p. 107). In restaurants, the usual garnish of Chicken Marengo consists of not only mushrooms and croûtons, but of 4 shelled Dublin prawns, or large *écrevisses*, and 4 small fried eggs. The pickling onions are omitted.

CHICKEN SAUTÉ WITH MUSHROOMS

Joint the chicken, season with salt and pepper, and cook to a golden colour in hot oil in a deep frying pan. When done, drain thoroughly, and put on a hot dish. Pour away most of the oil from the pan (but do not rinse the pan), add 1 table-spoon of finely-chopped shallots, stir and cook for a few minutes, then stir in 6 tablespoons of white wine, and boil till reduced by half. Add 2 ozs. of butter and pour this sauce over the pieces of chicken. Garnish with 1 lb. of mushrooms cooked as in recipe Mushrooms à la Bordelaise (see p. 28), and sprinkle with chopped parsley.

CHICKEN STUFFED WITH MUSHROOMS

Stuff the chicken with Mushroom Stuffing (see p. 72) and roast it, basting frequently with butter. Serve with a White Mushroom Sauce (see p. 66).

DUCK EN DODINE

Ingredients: 1 large duckling, 2 large onions, 2 small glasses of brandy, 1 pint of claret, 3½ ozs. of pork fat, 1 large tablespoon of olive oil, a few sprigs of parsley, thyme, a small bayleaf, 1 clove of garlic, ¾ lb. of small mushrooms, salt and pepper.

Method: Joint the duck, put it in an earthenware casserole and season with salt, pepper and mixed spices. Add the sliced onions, the herbs, brandy and red wine. Let stand for a few hours. Now put the oil and pork fat in another casserole and, when hot, put in the pieces of duck, which should have been carefully dried in a cloth. Cook for about 15 to 20 minutes, till equally browned on all sides. Add the wine, etc., in which the the duck has marinated, and the garlic. Simmer on a very gentle fire or in the oven, with the lid on the casserole, for 1 to 1½ hours. Half an hour before serving, put the peeled mushrooms in the casserole. This dish should be highly seasoned with salt and pepper. Serve in the casserole, with plain *nouilles* (flat ribbon macaroni), previously boiled, drained, tossed in a little butter and seasoned with salt and pepper.

PIGEONS EN SALMIS

Ingredients: For 2 or 3 pigeons: For the sauce: 1 oz. of butter and just under 1 oz. of flour, ¾ pint of veal or beef stock; 1 oz. each of carrots, onions, shallots, mushroom peelings, a few sprigs of parsley, thyme, a small bayleaf, 1 oz. of butter; 1½ gills of white wine, 4 tablespoons of brandy, 1 oz. of butter to finish the sauce, ¾ lb. of small mushrooms, 6 large croûtons of fried bread.

Method: Have ready two small saucepans, one for making the Brown Sauce, the other for the chopped vegetables and the carcasses of the pigeons. For making the sauce, melt the butter, stir in the flour and stir till brown. Then add the hot stock gradually, stirring continuously, and let simmer very gently till required. Lightly brown the chopped vegetables and herbs in butter. Roast the pigeons, basting them frequently. When nearly done, remove from the oven, and let stand for a few minutes. Then carve the birds, removing all the flesh from the bones. Put the pieces of pigeon in a saucepan, moisten with the hot brandy, cover the pan and keep warm. Break up the carcasses of the birds and pound them in a mortar. Add them to the vegetables, with the white wine, and on a brisk fire reduce to half the quantity. Then simmer for about 20 minutes, skimming carefully. Five minutes before serving, strain half the sauce over the pieces of pigeon, and put the saucepan on a slow fire, but without allowing to boil. Remove the saucepan containing the remainder of the sauce from the fire, and add 1 oz. of butter, divided into small pieces, and strain over the pigeons. Put on a hot dish and surround with the mushrooms, cooked as for a Garnish (see p. 38).

TURKEY WITH MUSHROOMS

Ingredients: 1 turkey, weighing about 10 lbs., ¾ lb. of lean veal, ¾ lb. of fat and lean pork, 6 ozs. of soft bread, soaked in milk and pressed, 1 lb. of chopped mushrooms and mushroom peelings and stalks, prepared as for Duxelles Sauce (see p. 64), ½ oz. of salt, a little pepper and grated nutmeg. For the Garnish: 1¼ lbs. of lean gammon, cut into dice, 2 lbs. of small button mushrooms. For the cooking of the turkey: 3 ozs. of chopped carrots, the same of onions, a few sprigs of parsley, thyme, 1 bayleaf, ¼ lb. of butter, ½ pint of stock.

Method: Mix the chopped veal, pork, bread and mushrooms, mushroom peelings and stalks, and cook lightly in a little butter, seasoning with salt, pepper and nutmeg. Stuff the turkey with the mixture. Now put the turkey in a thick saucepan over the chopped vegetables and herbs, pour the melted butter over it, cover the pan, and simmer in a slow oven, basting frequently and allowing 20 minutes to the pound. When nearly done, remove the lid, so that the bird may brown lightly. Now put the turkey in another saucepan, with the gammon, cut into dice, blanched and lightly coloured in hot butter, and the mushrooms, also browned in butter. Add the hot stock to the vegetables in the other pan, bring to the boil, reduce rapidly, and strain over the turkey. Cover the pan and cook for another 10 to 15 minutes. To serve, put the turkey on a hot dish, carve it, surround with the garnish, and either put the sauce over it or serve separately in a sauceboat.

TURKEY STUFFED WITH MUSHROOMS AND OYSTERS

Stuff the turkey with Mushroom and Oyster Stuffing (see p. 72), dredge it with salt, pour melted butter over it and roast it, allowing 20 minutes to the pound. Baste frequently with butter. Serve with a white Mushroom Sauce (see p. 66).

Game

CIVET OF HARE

Divide a young hare into neat joints. Brown $\frac{1}{4}$ lb. of gammon, cut into dice of about $\frac{1}{2}$ inch, in $1\frac{1}{2}$ ozs. of butter and the same quantity of pork fat. When browned, remove from the saucepan or earthenware casserole. In the same fat, brown 2 medium-sized onions, cut into quarters. When done, take out of the pan and put in the pieces of hare. Colour equally on all sides, then sprinkle with a little flour, mix well and, when brown, add $1\frac{1}{2}$ pints of stock and 4 tablespoons of vinegar (or the stock can be replaced by red wine, and the vinegar omitted). Stir, bring to the boil, add the gammon, the onions, a herb bouquet, a few peppercorns, and 1 level tablespoon of salt, if the stock is not sufficiently salted. Cover and simmer very gently in the oven for 2 to $2\frac{1}{2}$ hours. To serve, skim the sauce carefully, put the pieces of hare on a hot dish, strain the sauce over them, and garnish with the diced gammon, and $\frac{3}{4}$ lb. of small mushrooms, cooked as for a Garnish (see p. 38).

HARE À LA NIÇOISE

Joint the hare and brown the pieces in butter in an earthenware casserole. Season with salt and pepper, cover with $1\frac{1}{2}$ pints of red wine and a small glass of brandy. Cover and simmer very gently in the oven for 1½ to 2 hours. Half an hour before serving, add 6 or 8 small sausages, lightly browned in butter, and 1 lb. of small mushrooms. Finish cooking, and serve in the casserole.

HAZEL HENS WITH CREAM AND MUSHROOMS

Put 2½ ozs. of butter in an earthenware saucepan and, when hot, put in 2 hazel hens and baste them with the hot butter. Cover and simmer for 10 minutes in the oven, seasoning with salt and pepper. Then add ¾ pint of hot cream, and 4 dozen small button mushrooms. Cover and simmer till the hazel hens are quite tender. This will take from 30 to 40 minutes. Remove the hazel hens from the casserole, divide in half, replace them in the saucepan, add a squeeze of lemon juice, and serve in the casserole.

SALMIS OF QUAILS OR SNIPE

Roast the quails or snipe in a brisk oven for 15 to 20 minutes only, basting frequently with butter. Carve them when done, removing the breast, the legs and wings. Put them in a casserole, with 1 wineglass of Madeira, cover and keep warm. Chop the carcass, with the liver, heart, etc., of the birds, and put in a small saucepan with 2 chopped shallots, a bayleaf, a sprig of thyme, 1 clove of garlic and ½ pint of red wine. Bring to the boil and reduce by half. Then add 1 or 2 tablespoons of stock, and simmer very gently for about 20 minutes, stirring occasionally and seasoning with salt and pepper. Strain over the birds, and garnish with ¾ lb. of small mushrooms, previously cooked in butter, and well seasoned.

MUSHROOM AND GAME RISSOLES

Chop equal quantities of cooked game and cooked mushrooms, and bind with a little thick Duxelles Sauce (see p. 64). Roll out some puff pastry very thinly, and cut out in rounds of 4 inches in diameter. Put a little of the mixture on each round of pastry, fold over, damping and pressing the edges, so that the rissoles will not open when cooked, and either fry in a pan of deep very hot oil or fat, or bake in a quick oven to a light golden colour. They should be very crisp and served very hot.

PARTRIDGE À LA LAUTREC

Prepare the partridge for grilling by flattening it out and skewering it. Season with salt, brush over with melted butter, and grill somewhat slowly. When done, put on a hot dish and surround with small grilled mushrooms, moistened with a little butter, mixed with chopped parsley and lemon juice and well seasoned with salt and pepper. Sprinkle the partridge with lemon juice.

PHEASANT EN COCOTE

Cover the pheasant with strips of larding bacon
and tie. Put it in an earthenware casserole with
$\frac{1}{4}$ lb. of butter, and season well with salt and
pepper. Cover, put in the oven and cook very
slowly, basting frequently, for about $\frac{3}{4}$ hour to
1 hour or longer, according to the size of the bird.
Twenty minutes before serving, add $\frac{3}{4}$ lb. of
small mushrooms, lightly cooked in butter, 18
pickling onions, also cooked in butter, and a few
truffles (optional). To serve, put the pheasant on
a hot dish, remove the larding bacon, carve the
bird, surround with the garnish. Strain over it
the butter in which it was cooked.

STUFFED PHEASANT EN COCOTE

Stuff the pheasant with a Mushroom Stuffing
(see p. 72) and cook it as in the foregoing recipe.
Omit the mushroom and onion and truffle garnish, and serve with a Duxelles Sauce (see p. 64).

GIBELOTTE OF RABBIT

Ingredients: A young rabbit, weighing from 5
to 6 lbs., $\frac{1}{2}$ lb. of lean gammon, 18 pickling
onions, 1 lb. of mushrooms, 1 tablespoon of flour,
$\frac{3}{4}$ pint of white wine, $\frac{1}{2}$ pint of stock, lard, butter
or oil, 1 clove of garlic, salt and pepper.

Method: Carve the rabbit into neat joints. Melt
a few tablespoons of lard, butter or oil in a sauce-

pan and, when hot, add the pieces of rabbit and season with salt and pepper. Cook till equally browned on all sides. Sprinkle with the flour and let this brown also. Then add the wine and stock, bring to the boil, cover and simmer for $\frac{1}{2}$ hour. Now add the bacon, cut into dice, the onions, both having been lightly browned in butter, and the mushrooms and garlic. Cover and simmer for another $\frac{1}{2}$ hour. Serve on a somewhat deep dish, with the garnish and a few croûtons of fried bread.

RABBIT EN COCOTE WITH MUSHROOMS

This is done in the same manner as Chicken En Cocote with Mushrooms (see p. 113).

QUALITY PAPERBACK BOOKS
Designed to Instruct and Entertain
Each book written by an expert in his field

Acting and Stage Movement, 95¢

Aeromodeling, $1.45

Amateur Psychologist's
Dictionary, 95¢

Antique Furniture for the Smaller
Home, 95¢

Archery, 95¢

Art of Riding, 95¢

Astrology, 95¢

Boy or Girl? Names for Every
Child, 95¢

Cheiro's Book of Numbers, 95¢

Cheiro's Palmistry for All, 95¢

Cheiro's When Were You Born?, 95¢

Complete Guide to Palmistry, 95¢

Drama, 95¢

Find Your Job and Land It, 95¢

Fitness After Forty, $1.45

Gift Wrapping, 95¢

Golf at a Glance, 95¢

Guide to Personality Through
Handwriting, $1.45

Health Foods and Herbs, 95¢

Heart Disease and High Blood
Pressure, 95¢

Home Brewing Without Failures, 95¢

How to Be Healthy With Yoga, 95¢

How to Beat Personality Tests, $1.45

How to Train for Track and Field, 95¢

How to Win at Gin Rummy, 95¢

Instant Etiquette for
Businessmen, 95¢

Judo and Self Defense, 95¢

Knots and Splices, 95¢

Laughter in a Damp Climate, $1.45

Lawn Tennis, 95¢

Magic of Numbers, 95¢

Manual of Sex and Marriage, $1.45

Mas Oyama's Karate, 95¢

Muscle Building for Beginners, 95¢

Mushroom Recipes, $1.45

131 Magic Tricks for Amateurs, 95¢

Painting and Drawing, 95¢

Practical Guide to Antique
Collecting, 95¢

Production & Staging of Plays, 95¢

Profitable Poker, $1.45

Public Speaking, $1.45

Radio Astronomy and Building Your
Own Telescope, 95¢

Remembering Made Easy, 95¢

Sailing Step by Step, 95¢

Shakespeare in the Red, 95¢

She Looks at Sex, 95¢

Slipped Discs, 95¢

Stamp Collecting for Fun and
Profit, $1.45

Stomach Ulcers, 95¢

Student's Guide, $1.45

Successful Winemaking at Home, 95¢

3 Great Classics, $1.45

Upholstery, 95¢

Wake Up and Write, 95¢

Weightlifting & Weight Training, 95¢

Whole Truth About Allergy, 95¢

Woodturning, 95¢

You and Your Dog, 95¢

You Can Find a Fortune, $1.45

Your Allergic Child, $1.45

All books are also available in cloth-bound library editions at $2.50 and $3.50. If your bookstore is out of stock on any of the above titles, you can order books directly from ARC BOOKS, Inc., 219 Park Avenue South, New York, N.Y. 10003. Enclose check or money order for list price of books plus 10¢ per book for postage and handling. No C.O.D.